ENCOUNTERS IN YELLOWSTONE

The Nez Perce Summer of 1877

M. MARK MILLER

TWODOT®

GUILFORD, CONNECTICUT
HELENA, MONTANA

A · TWODOT® · BOOK

An imprint and registered trademark of The Rowman & Littlefield Publishing Group, Inc.
4501 Forbes Blvd., Ste. 200
Lanham, MD 20706
www.rowman.com

Distributed by NATIONAL BOOK NETWORK

Copyright © 2019 by M. Mark Miller

All rights reserved. No part of this book may be reproduced in any form or by any electronic or mechanical means, including information storage and retrieval systems, without written permission from the publisher, except by a reviewer who may quote passages in a review.

British Library Cataloguing in Publication Information available

Library of Congress Cataloging-in-Publication Data available

ISBN 978-1-4930-4520-4 (paperback)
ISBN 978-1-4930-4521-1 (e-book)

♾™ The paper used in this publication meets the minimum requirements of American National Standard for Information Sciences—Permanence of Paper for Printed Library Materials, ANSI/NISO Z39.48-1992.

This book is dedicated to my lifelong friend Ralph Schmidt, whose prodigious knowledge of Yellowstone Park and willingness to consult maps and calendars to get the facts right did so much to improve this book.

CONTENTS

Map of Events outside Yellowstone Park. vi
Map of Events inside Yellowstone Park vii
Cast of Characters ix
Timeline xv
Preface xviii

Chapter 1 — The Magnetic Cabin. 1
Chapter 2 — General Sherman's Trip 5
Chapter 3 — Radersburg to Geyserland. 14
Chapter 4 — Scouts Search for the Nez Perce. 29
Chapter 5 — The Reluctant Guide 37
Chapter 6 — Frolic in Geyserland. 44
Chapter 7 — Radersburg Capture 57
Chapter 8 — Joe Roberts's Adventure 68
Chapter 9 — A Decent Burial. 79
Chapter 10 — Captivity and Release 92
Chapter 11 — Ben Stone Escapes 108
Chapter 12 — George's Ordeal 116

Acknowledgments 130
Endnotes. 131
References 139
Index 142
About the Author 151

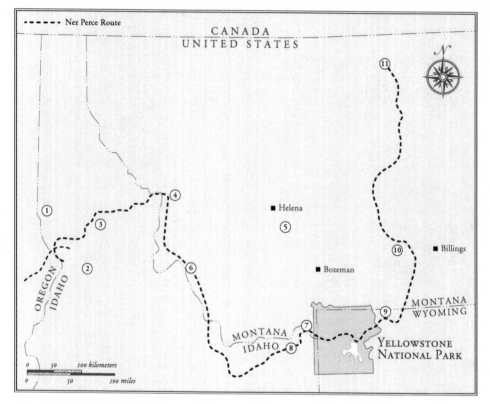

- - - - - Nez Perce Route

CANADA
UNITED STATES

■ Helena

■ Billings

■ Bozeman

OREGON
IDAHO

MONTANA
WYOMING

MONTANA
IDAHO

YELLOWSTONE
NATIONAL PARK

0   50   100 kilometers
0   50   100 miles

Key to Map of Events outside Yellowstone Park

1. May 15-19, 1877: General O. O. Howard meets with non-treaty Nez Perce at Lapwai, Idaho, and orders the Indians to move to a reservation.

2. June 12, 1877: Young Indians are provoked into attacking settlers and widespread hostilities break out.

3. July 5, 1877: Non-treaty Nez Perce decide to abandon their homeland and head to the Montana plains.

4. July 28, 1877: Nez Perce bypass army barricades at Fort Fizzle in Lolo Canyon west of Missoula.

5. August 5, 1877: The Radersburg Party leaves that town bound for Yellowstone Park.

6. August 9-10, 1877: Colonel John Gibbon launches dawn attack on sleeping Nez Perce camp on the banks of the Big Hole River.

7. August 10, 1877: The Radersburg Party makes camp at Henrys Lake.

8. August 20, 1877: Nez Perce raid General Howard's camp at Camas Meadows and make off with 150 mules.

9. September 5, 1877: Nez Perce elude the Seventh Cavalry under Colonel Samuel Sturgis and leave Yellowstone Park.

10. September 13, 1877: The Nez Perce repel pursuing cavalry at the Battle of Canyon Creek.

11. October 5, 1877: The last remaining leader of the Nez Perce, Chief Joseph, surrenders the remnants of the tribe after the Battle of Bear Paw.

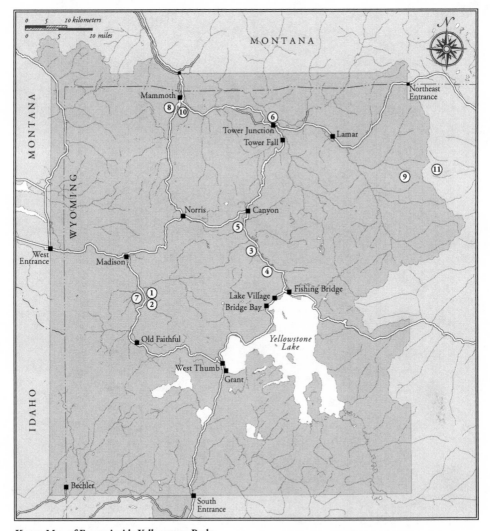

Key to Map of Events inside Yellowstone Park

① August 23, 1877: Nez Perce scouts under Yellow Wolf capture prospector John Shively and force him to guide them through Yellowstone Park.

② August 24, 1877: The Nez Perce capture the Radersburg Party and shoot two of the men along Nez Perce Creek.

③ August 25, 1877: Nez Perce set Emma Cowan and her siblings, Frank and Ida Carpenter, free in the Yellowstone wilderness.

④ August 25, 1877: Recently discharged soldier James C. Irwin is captured in Hayden Valley and inadvertently betrays the presence of the Helena Party.

⑤ August 26, 1877: Nez Perce scouts attack the Helena Party killing Charles Kenck and driving the rest into the wilderness.

⑥ August 27, 1877: Army scouts find Emma Cowan, Ida and Frank Carpenter and take them to McCartney's cabin at Mammoth Hot Springs.

⑦ September 2, 1877: George Cowan is picked up by General O. O. Howard's scouts.

⑧ August 31, 1877: Nez Perce scouts under YellowWolf attack McCartney's cabin at Mammoth Hot Springs killing Richard Dietrich and sending Ben Stone into hiding.

⑨ September 5, 1877: John Shively slips away from the Nez Perce camp near Lamar Valley.

⑩ September 5, 1877: John Shively arrives at Mammoth Hot Springs and finds McCartney's cabin abandoned.

⑪ September 5, 1877: The Nez Perce elude the army and leave Yellowstone Park.

CAST OF CHARACTERS

RADERSBURG PARTY

Nine tourists from Helena and Radersburg, then the seat of Jefferson County, Montana, left Radersburg on August 5, 1877, and made their way up the Missouri and Madison river valleys. After a three-day stop at Henrys Lake, they continued to the park on August 10. After several days of sightseeing, they were preparing to depart on August 24 when Indians accosted them, shooting two men and taking two women and their brother captive.

A. J. Arnold, thirty-seven, a store clerk from the town of Blackfoot near Helena. George Cowan credited Arnold with saving his life after the army rescued the two men.

Frank Carpenter, twenty-seven, a mining engineer from Helena. Brother of Ida Carpenter and Emma Cowan. Frank was the organizer of the Radersburg Party. After the Nez Perce released Frank and his sisters from captivity, he led them through the park. He published a highly colored book about his adventures in 1878.

Ida Carpenter, thirteen, sister of Frank Carpenter and Emma Cowan. The Nez Perce took Ida, Frank, and Emma captive on August 24.

Emma Cowan, twenty-two, wife of George Cowan; sister of Ida and Frank Carpenter. The Nez Perce took Emma, Frank, and Ida captive on August 24. Emma's memoir about her adventure was published in 1908. It is a much-anthologized gem of Montana literature.

George Cowan, thirty-five, Jefferson County attorney from Radersburg. Husband of Emma Cowan. Indians shot George and left him for dead on August 24. He couldn't walk, so he crawled for several days before scouts found him. The army then hauled him across the roadless wilderness in a wagon.

William Dingee, forty-two, saloon keeper from Helena.

Charles Mann, eighteen, Jefferson County deputy clerk. An artist who sketched scenes throughout the trip and planned to write a book about it.

Henry Meyers, a young man hired by George Cowan to drive the supply wagon.

Albert Oldham, thirty-seven, a friend of Frank Carpenter from Helena.

Helena Party

A group of ten men from Helena who assembled at Mammoth Hot Springs on August 22, 1877. The members made their way to a point south of the Yellowstone Falls where they saw the Nez Perce crossing the Yellowstone River on August 25 and went into hiding. The next day, Nez Perce scouts attacked their camp, killing Charles Kenck and scattering the rest into the wilderness. Most of the survivors made for Mammoth Hot Springs, but two teenagers fled southward through the Yellowstone wilderness.

Richard Dietrich, twenty-four, a popular German-born music teacher from Helena. Dietrich was killed when Nez Perce scouts attacked at McCartney's cabin at Mammoth Hot Springs on August 31.

Leander Duncan, thirty, a mine owner from Helena.

August Foller, sixteen, the son of a brewer from Helena. After Nez Perce scouts attacked the Helena Party camp on August 26, Foller fled southward through Yellowstone Park with Joe Roberts. They were rescued by teamsters on the Madison River and went home by stagecoach from Virginia City. Some accounts confuse young Gus with his forty-six-year-old father.

Charles Kenck, thirty-seven, proprietor of a brewery in Helena. Killed August 26, 1877, in a Nez Perce raid. The only married man in the Helena Party, Kenck left a widow and two children.

Frederic Pfister, twenty-seven, furniture dealer from Helena.

Joseph Roberts, nineteen, son of a prominent Helena family. Roberts and August Foller fled southward through the park after Nez Perce scouts attack the Helena Party camp on August 26.

John Stewart, thirty-seven, affiliated with New Helena Water Company. Seriously wounded in the August 26, 1877, attack on the Helena Party.

Ben Stone, forty-four, African American cook for the Helena Party. Stone waited at McCartney's cabin to help his companions when they returned. He fled when Indian scouts attacked there.

Andrew Weikert, thirty-one, owner of a mine near Helena. Weikert left the Helena Party camp with Leslie Wilkie on August 26, 1877, to locate the Nez Perce and returned to find Indian scouts had attacked his companions. After helping several of his companions return to Mammoth Hot Springs, Weikert returned to the wilderness with James McCartney to find others. Indians attacked them on their return. After recovering from his wounds, Weikert went back to the park to recover the bodies of companions killed by the Indians.

Leslie Wilkie, twenty-seven, clerk at the Montana Territorial Surveyor Generals Office in Helena.

SOLDIERS AND SCOUTS

The army sent units from across the northwest from Washington State to the Dakotas to find and subdue the Nez Perce and hired civilian scouts to aid in the effort.

Jack Bean, thirty-three, a trapper, hunter, and Yellowstone Park guide. The army hired Bean and another Indian fighter, George Herendeen, to find out if the Nez Perce were going toward Montana settlements or into Yellowstone Park.

Lieutenant Gustavus Doane, thirty-seven, led a contingent of cavalry supplemented by about sixty Crow Indians up the Yellowstone River to contain the Nez Perce in Yellowstone Park.

Stanton G. Fisher, thirty-seven, a scout hired by the army to recruit Bannack Indians to pursue the Nez Perce. Fisher and his men entered Yellowstone Park ahead of General O. O. Howard's and found several survivors of Nez Perce attacks on tourists.

Colonel John Gibbon, forty, commander of the U.S. Army in Montana Territory. Gibbon assembled troops under his command and volunteers and led the attack on the Nez Perce at the Big Hole. The Indians repelled the army and fled.

George Herendeen, thirty-one, gained fame as a scout with Colonel George Armstrong Custer's ill-fated army that was defeated at the Battle of the Little Bighorn in 1876. Herendeen rode from the battlefield to Bismarck, North Dakota, and provided the first written account of the battle. In 1877 he went with Jack Bean to find out if the Nez Perce were headed toward Montana settlements or into Yellowstone Park.

General Oliver Otis Howard, a Civil War hero and commander of the Department of Columbia of the U.S. Army. General Howard ordered the Nez Perce onto a reservation and pursued them with his six-hundred-man army for more than a thousand miles.

Colonel Nelson Miles, thirty-eight, a Civil War veteran who led his troops on a forced march across Eastern Montana and intercepted the Nez Perce near the Bear Paw Mountains forty miles south of the Canadian border on September 30. The Indians surrendered on October 5 after a siege in winter weather.

Colonel O. M. Poe, fifty-four, one of General William Tecumseh Sherman's aides-de-camp. Poe provided a detailed account of Sherman's trip through Yellowstone Park.

Lieutenant Hugh Lenox Scott, twenty-four, accompanied Lieutenant Gustavus Doane on his mission to contain the Nez Perce in Yellowstone Park. Scott pursued Indian scouts who had attacked a ranch north of the park to Mammoth Hot Springs, where he found Richard Dietrich's body in McCartney's cabin.

General William Tecumseh Sherman, fifty-seven, is credited with breaking the will of the Confederacy by his march to the sea during the American Civil War. Sherman was commanding general of the entire U.S. Army in the summer of 1877 when he toured Yellowstone Park. He delegated efforts to pursue and capture the Nez Perce to his subordinates.

NEZ PERCE

Joseph, thirty-seven, chief of the Wallowa band of the Nez Perce, one of five bands that fled their homeland to avoid being forced onto a reservation. Many accounts erroneously say Chief Joseph was the supreme leader of the five bands and credit him with evading the army. He was an important member of the Nez Perce council of chiefs and the last chief available to surrender after the Battle of Bear Paw. He spent the remainder of his life arguing for justice for his people.

Looking Glass, forty-five, chief of the Alpowai band of Nez Perce. He was the leader of the Nez Perce during much of their flights.

Poker Joe, age unknown, was chief of a small band of Nez Perce. The council of chiefs chose him to lead the combined bands after the Big Hole Battle because of his knowledge of routes in Montana. He protected captive Yellowstone tourists and is credited with saving their lives.

White Bird, chief of the Lamatta band of Nez Perce.

Yellow Wolf, about twenty-two, a relative of Chief Joseph, who told his version of the flight of the Nez Perce to a white author over the objections of tribe members. The resulting book is one of few accounts of the events from an Indian perspective. Yellow Wolf was with the Nez Perce scouts who attacked McCartney's cabin on August 31 and killed Richard Dietrich.

OTHERS

Several others were in Yellowstone Park when the Nez Perce passed through in the summer of 1877.

Henry Buck, thirty-one, a merchant and teamster from Stevensville, Montana, who was pressed into service to drive freight and troops for General O. O. Howard. Buck crossed Yellowstone Park with Howard's army and helped the injured tourist George Cowan.

James C. Irwin, age unknown, a soldier recently discharged from Fort Ellis who was captured by the Nez Perce in Hayden Valley on August 25, 1877. Irwin inadvertently informed the Indians about the Helena Party that was later attacked by Nez Perce scouts.

William Harmon, age unknown, was a Colorado prospector who left the Nelson Story Party to join the Radersburg Party and was captured with them.

George Huston, a Yellowstone Park guide who had prospected for gold in the area for more than a decade. Huston met the Radersburg Party at the Lower Geyser Basin on August 17 and accompanied them to the Upper Basin. Later he guided Frank Carpenter and his friends to Yellowstone Lake and Canyon.

James McCartney, forty-one, claimed a homestead at Mammoth Hot Springs in 1871 and built a cabin there that served as a hotel for Yellowstone travelers. McCartney's cabin was a haven for tourists accosted by the Nez Perce. He accompanied Andrew Weikert on a search for missing members of the Helena Party, and they were attacked.

Texas Jack Omohundro, thirty-one, a scout, guide, and flamboyant showman who had performed in stage shows with Buffalo Bill Cody. Texas Jack guided two Englishmen on a hunting expedition in the park in 1877 and accompanied Emma Cowan and her siblings out of the park. After leaving the park, he immediately went on the road with his own Wild West show, which he promoted by telling newspaper reporters outlandish tales of rescuing park tourists.

John Shively, forty-one, a prospector who had searched for gold in Yellowstone Park for several weeks before being captured on August 23 by the Nez Perce and forced to guide them across the park. Shively befriended Emma Cowan and her siblings while they were in captivity. He was with the Indians for thirteen days.

Nelson Story, thirty-nine, a Bozeman businessman who made his fortune trailing a thousand longhorn cattle from Texas to the Montana gold rush in 1866. Story and his companions visited the Lower Geyser Basin on August 23, 1877. Apparently, they were the ones who Emma Cowan said informed the Radersburg Party about the Big Hole Battle, news she erroneously attributed to General Sherman's party.

TIMELINE

1877

May 15–19: General O. O. Howard and the chiefs of the nontreaty Nez Perce meet at Lapwai, Idaho. After Howard arrests their spokesman, the chiefs agree to comply with Howard's demand that they move to a reservation and go to choose allotments.

June 3: The nontreaty bands of Nez Perce convene at Tolo Lake to gather camas and hold a council.

June 13: Young Indians are provoked into attacking settlers. Widespread hostilities break out.

July 15: The nontreaty Nez Perce decide to abandon their homeland and head over Lolo Trail toward Montana after several battles with the army.

July 28: Nez Perce bypass army barricades at Fort Fizzle in Lolo Canyon west of Missoula.

August 4: General Sherman leaves Fort Ellis for Yellowstone Park.

August 5: Radersburg Party leaves that city for Yellowstone Park.

August 6: The Radersburg Party dines at the hotel in the town of Sterling, where they hear about "Indian troubles," but they decide to go on to the park.

August 7: The Nez Perce camp on the banks of the Big Hole River.

August 9–10: Colonel John Gibbon launches a dawn attack on the sleeping Nez Perce camp on the banks of the Big Hole River. Indians repel the attack and flee the next day.

August 10: The Radersburg Party arrives at Henrys Lake.

August 13: Colonel John Gibbon sends a telegram from Deer Lodge to Fort Ellis ordering officers to hire scouts to find the Nez Perce.

Jack Bean and George Herendeen leave Bozeman to search for the Nez Perce.

Andrew Weikert, Richard Dietrich, Fred Pfister, and Joe Roberts of the Helena Party depart that town for Yellowstone Park.

The Radersburg Party leaves Henrys Lake for the park.

August 16: General Sherman first hears news of the Big Hole Battle and rushes back to Fort Ellis the next day for more information.

August 18: General Sherman arrives back at Fort Ellis after meeting members of the Helena Party on their way to the park.

August 19: Frank Carpenter and his friends dump rubble down Old Faithful in an attempt to block it.

August 20: The Nez Perce raid General Howard's camp and Camas Meadows and make off with 150 mules.

August 22: The Helena Party assembles at Mammoth Hot Springs.

August 23: Yellow Wolf and his companions capture prospector John Shively and take him to the Nez Perce chiefs, who decide to force him to guide them through the park.

Nelson Story and his companions visit the Lower Geyser Basin and make a hasty retreat after telling the Radersburg Party about the Big Hole Battle.

After their trip to the park interior, Frank Carpenter and his friends join the rest of the Radersburg Party at the Lower Geyser Basin, and the group makes plans to return home.

Yellow Wolf sees the bonfire the Radersburg Party set to celebrate the end of their Yellowstone visit.

Scouts Jack Bean and George Herendeen send a telegram to the army reporting the Nez Perce are headed into Yellowstone Park.

August 24: The Nez Perce attack the Radersburg Party at the Lower Geyser Basin, shooting two men and leaving them for dead, and they capture a brother and two sisters and scatter the rest.

The Helena Party visits Yellowstone Falls.

August 25: The Helena Party sees the Nez Perce crossing the Yellowstone River in the Hayden Valley and flees to a secluded campsite.

The Nez Perce set Emma Cowan and Frank and Ida Carpenter free in the Yellowstone Park wilderness.

George and Emma Cowan's second wedding anniversary.

Recently discharged soldier James C. Irwin is captured by the Nez Perce in Hayden Valley and inadvertently lets the Indians know about the Helena Party.

August 26: Andrew Weikert and Leslie Wilkie leave the Helena Party camp to see if the Nez Perce have gone. They return to find the camp looted and deserted.

Nez Perce scouts attack the Helena Party camp, killing Charles Kenck and driving others into the wilderness.

August 27: Army scouts find Emma Cowan and Ida and Frank Carpenter and take them to McCartney's cabin at Mammoth Hot Springs.

Survivors of the Nez Perce attack on the Helena Party straggle back to McCartney's cabin.

August 28: Andrew Weikert and James McCartney leave Mammoth Hot Springs to search for missing members of the Helena Party.

August 30: George Cowan is picked up by Howard's scouts.

Joe Roberts and August Foller of the Helena Party, and Henry Meyers and William Dingee of the Radersburg Party, arrive in Virginia City.

August 31: Nez Perce scouts attack McCartney's cabin at Mammoth Hot Springs, killing Richard Dietrich and sending Ben Stone into hiding.

September 2: John Shively slips away from the Nez Perce near the Lamar Valley.

September 5: John Shively arrives at McCartney's deserted cabin at Mammoth Hot Springs but doesn't find Richard Dietrich's body, which is buried nearby.

Nez Perce elude the army and depart Yellowstone Park.

October 5: Chief Joseph surrenders the remnants of the Nez Perce after a long siege in winter weather.

October 11: Andrew Weikert returns to Yellowstone Park and recovers Richard Dietrich's body, but deep snow keeps him from recovering Charles Kenck's body.

October 28: The Helena Gesang Verein harmonica society holds a funeral for Richard Dietrich.

PREFACE

On September 29, 1877, several inches of snow fell on the Montana plains where five bands of Nez Perce (pronounced Nez PURSE) were camped and resting after a twelve-hundred-mile running battle with the U.S. Army. The Indians were fleeing to Canada where they hoped to join the Lakota chief, Sitting Bull, who had gone there after his warriors decimated Colonel George Armstrong Custer's Seventh Cavalry at the Battle of the Little Big Horn the year before. The Nez Perce's plan to make a new life in Montana failed when the Crow Indians refused their request to settle there. The Nez Perce had outmaneuvered, outfought, and outsmarted armies pursuing them from the west over and over, but they were about to be intercepted by an army approaching from the east.

On September 30, Cheyenne scouts found the Nez Perce camp and told their commander, Colonel Nelson A. Miles, where it was. Miles feared the Nez Perce would escape as they had several times before, so he immediately ordered an attack. He hoped his mounted soldiers' onslaught would frighten the Indians into disarray and they would be subdued quickly. But this strategy failed, just as it had when Colonel John Gibbon attacked the Nez Perce on the banks of the Big Hole River in western Montana on the previous August 9. The Indians rallied and drove Miles's attackers back. Then the opponents settled in for a siege.

Both sides dug in and continued exchanging shots. The Nez Perce hoped—and Colonel Miles feared—that Sitting Bull would send his Sioux warriors south from Canada to rescue the Nez Perce. That never happened, but one of the Nez Perce chiefs, Looking Glass, was shot dead by a sniper when he raised up to look for approaching Lakota reinforcements.

Colonel Miles did get reinforcements when General Oliver Otis Howard arrived with his six-hundred-man army that had chased the Nez Perce all the way from Idaho. Joseph, who was the last remaining chief of the Nez Perce bands, decided to surrender and gave his famous speech:

Tell General Howard I know his heart. What he told me before I have in my heart. I am tired of fighting. Our chiefs are killed. Looking Glass is dead. Toohoolhoolzote is dead. The old men are all dead. It is the young men who say yes or no. He who led the young men is dead. It is cold and we have no blankets. The little children are freezing to death. My people, some of them, have run away to the hills, and have no blankets, no food; no one knows where they are—perhaps freezing to death. I want to have time to look for my children and see how many of them I can find. Maybe I shall find them among the dead. Hear me, my chiefs. I am tired; my heart is sick and sad. From where the sun now stands I will fight no more forever.

Chief Joseph's surrender marked the end of the last battle of what has been called the last Indian war.

* * * *

The flight of the Nez Perce is an iconic American story. Its outline is clear. Indians befriend whites and live amicably with them for decades. Then gold is discovered on Indian land. Prospectors rush in and settlers follow. Tensions mount, and finally the government forces the Indians off their land at gunpoint.

For the Nez Perce, this story began on September 20, 1804, when starving members of the famous Lewis and Clark Expedition staggered into a Nez Perce camp. The Indians fed the explorers, provided them with horses, and sent them on their westward journey to the Pacific. When the explorers return the next spring, the Indians promised to live in peace with whites—a promise they kept until violence erupted in the summer of 1877.

By the summer of 1836, Presbyterian missionaries had arrived in Nez Perce country. Some Nez Perce bands embraced Christianity, while others retained their traditional ways. The split widened in 1863 when the government announced a treaty had been negotiated with a Nez Perce chief called Lawyer. The Christian Nez Perce agreed to settle on a newly defined reservation, but the non-Christian bands didn't recognize Lawyer as their leader and stayed on their traditional lands. The government called the holdouts the "nontreaty Nez Perce."

After gold was discovered on nontreaty Nez Perce land in 1860, prospectors rushed in, and farmers and ranchers followed them. At first the Indians tolerated settlers, but in the summer of 1876 a white man killed a Nez Perce

General Oliver Otis Howard led an army of six hundred men in pursuit of the Nez Perce for 1,200 miles from the Indians homeland on the Idaho-Washington border to the final battle near the Bear Paw Mountains in central Montana.

LIBRARY OF CONGRESS

man in the Wallowa Valley. Later the murderer was acquitted. Tensions continued to rise, and settlers demanded that the government remove the Indians to the reservation that was defined in the 1860 treaty.

In May 1877 General Oliver Otis Howard convened a "peace council" at Fort Lapwai, Idaho, and ordered the nontreaty Nez Perce to move to the reservation in thirty days. Toohoolhoolzote, the chief of a small band that the Nez Perce had chosen to speak for them, adamantly refused the ultimatum, so the exasperated General Howard had him arrested. The other chiefs then acquiesced and went with Howard to choose allotments on the reservation. Afterward, the chiefs returned to their homelands and told their people to begin rounding up their cattle and horses and preparing to move.

In June several nontreaty bands gathered at Tolo Lake for traditional games and to gather camas root for food one last time. There a young brave was goaded into taking revenge on the white man who had murdered his father the year before. He recruited his cousins to join him and began killing settlers. Widespread hostilities broke out.

On July 1 volunteers accompanying soldiers fired shots at a peaceful Nez Perce band under Chief White Bird, who was approaching them under a truce flag. White Bird then decided to join the nontreaty Nez Perce bands. After several fights, the Indians saw that General Howard was amassing a huge army, so they decided to abandon their homeland and head to the buffalo country on the Montana plains in hopes of making a new life. They headed east over the Lolo Trail toward Montana.

The Nez Perce bypassed barricades in Lolo Canyon by taking their whole party—including women, children, and elderly, and a herd of fifteen hundred horses—over a mountain that the army thought was impassable. The Indians had quit negotiations with the army and made a side agreement with white settlers that they would travel peacefully through Montana to the buffalo country on the plains. They honored that agreement until Colonel John Gibbon ordered his troops to launch a dawn attack on them on the banks of the Big Hole River. After the Nez Perce repelled Gibbon's attack, the Indians fled. They chose a route to minimize contact with white settlers and the army. That route took them through the newly established Yellowstone National Park. After outmaneuvering the army to escape the park, the Indians fought their way across the Montana plains to their final defeat by Colonel Miles at the Battle of Bear Paw.

* * * *

There is a long list of books that describe and explain the Nez Perce flight from its beginning near the Oregon, Washington, and Idaho state lines to its tragic end in the northern Montana plains. This book focuses on a single phase of that travail, a phase that has not received sufficient attention—the stories of tourists who tangled with the Nez Perce when the Indians made their way across Yellowstone National Park.

There is no fiction here. No names have been changed, no characters invented, no events fabricated. These stories adhere to the facts as they can be documented or reasonably inferred. They come primarily from first-person accounts by the people who lived the adventures.

Tourists' encounters with the Nez Perce in Yellowstone Park generated enormous interest in the summer of 1877, so Montana territorial newspapers were eager to interview people when they returned to civilization. Newspapers also published the accounts of those able and willing to write them. A steady stream of journals and reminiscences by people who were in the park that summer appeared for another sixty years.

Books about the flight of the Nez Perce began appearing in 1878 when Frank Carpenter published an account of his adventures in Yellowstone Park titled *The Wonders of Geyser Land*. Carpenter's book is marred by his efforts to add interest by making up anecdotes and presenting himself as a hero. Similarly, General Oliver Otis Howard's 1880 book, *Nez Perce Joseph*, apparently was written hastily from memory. It is riddled with factual errors, not the least of which is his portrayal of Chief Joseph as the primary leader of the Indians. Howard seems to have wanted to paint Chief Joseph as a military genius to justify the army's many humiliating defeats by the Nez Perce. All of this is to say that my book is based on a rich vein of first-person accounts that were treated with skepticism. When things appeared to me to be implausible, I omitted them. For example, Frank Carpenter's reports of Nez Perce talking to each other in pidgin English probably never happened, so I disregarded them. I cross-checked sources whenever possible, and when only one source was available I used it with caution.

Often what appeared to be conflicts in accounts sprang from people's literally being in different places and therefore seeing things differently. Scrutiny of accounts resolved most of these conflicts, and that resulted in more detailed and compelling stories. When such conflicts could not be resolved, I chose a version that I thought comported best with the facts without comment. I am a storyteller, not a historian, and I didn't want to mar my narrative with a lot of "he said/she said" statements.

Anything enclosed in quotation marks in these stories comes from material written by the person being quoted (or by people they quoted). Of course, the direct quotations are the reconstructions of their authors. No one remembers the exact words of all their conversations, particularly in stressful situations like being surrounded by hostile forces.

Throughout I have used place names as they are recognized in 2018 so today's readers can determine where actions took place. However, I have tried to describe geothermal and geological features as they appeared in 1877. For example, Mud Volcano was hurling gobs of mud in 1877 but is now a quiet spring.

In this era, white people often called individual Indians by several names. For example, the man who was in charge of the Nez Perce while they were in Yellowstone Park was variously known as "Poker Joe," "Joe Hale," or "Lean Elk." To avoid confusion, I have used just one name for such men, "Poker Joe" in this case.

During the Civil War, many officers held brevet ranks but returned to lower ranks when hostilities ceased. In this book I have used the ranks such officers held after the war. George Armstrong Custer, John Gibbon, and Nelson Miles held the rank of colonel in the period described.

While preparing this book, I consulted a number of secondary sources and occasionally found errors in them, but I decided to leave it to historians to correct the record. Nitpicking details invites scrutiny, and I am painfully aware of how easy it is to make mistakes. My editors and I have found I made plenty of errors during preparations of this manuscript and corrected them. But despite everyone's efforts, errors always creep in. Of course, I take responsibility for any mistakes that remain.

CHAPTER 1

The Magnetic Cabin

On August 1877 a log cabin northwest of the Liberty Cap at Mammoth Hot Springs attracted travelers from all over Yellowstone Park like a magnet. The twenty-by-thirty-foot log structure had a dirt floor and a sod roof and was nestled in Clematis Gulch. In a park that covered nearly 3,500 square miles, it was the only inhabited building. An early traveler described the primitive little cabin as "the last outpost of civilization."[1] By that he meant it was the last place a person could buy whiskey before entering the roadless Yellowstone wilderness. Yellowstone pioneer James McCartney had built the cabin and several crude bathhouses in 1871 to create a resort. At a time when most hot water was heated in a tea kettle on a wood stove, people flocked to natural hot springs spas that offered never-ending baths.

But in the summer of 1877 tourists weren't coming to McCartney's to enjoy the baths. They rushed there to escape hostile Nez Perce Indians who had attacked their camps and killed their companions. The beleaguered travelers hoped to find food, rest, and someone to bind their wounds.

The Indians were fleeing through Yellowstone Park after several fierce battles with the army, which was trying to force them to leave their homeland near the intersection of the Idaho, Washington, and Oregon state lines. Rather than go to a new reservation, five Nez Perce bands decided to try for a new life in the buffalo country on the eastern Montana plains. They chose to travel through the park to avoid populated areas of western Montana, but there were a few hapless tourists there.

* * * *

William Tecumseh Sherman, the Civil War general whose famous March to the Sea broke the back of the Confederacy, finished a whirlwind tour of the park and left McCartney's cabin just before the Indians arrived there. Although Sherman knew that six hundred Nez Perce had entered Montana, he traveled to the park with a party of only ten men. He was commanding general of the entire U.S. Army so he could have had as many men as he wanted, but he was sure the Indians were afraid of geysers and wouldn't enter Yellowstone Park. Also, he wanted to leave as many men as possible to capture the Nez Perce.

Shortly after Sherman left McCartney's, Texas Jack Omohundro, a flamboyant showman and sometime partner of Buffalo Bill Cody, arrived there. He raced to McCartney's when he discovered the Nez Perce marauding in the park. He didn't even pause to tell other tourists he passed the Indians were coming. Texas Jack just rounded up the two Englishmen he was guiding on a hunting trip and ran. One of his clients was a physician who would get a chance to practice his profession over the next few days by treating wounded and bedraggled tourists who straggled to McCartney's after gun battles with the Indians.

While Texas Jack and his companions lolled around McCartney's cabin, the Nez Perce were preparing to break camp at Henrys Lake about sixty miles to the southwest. The main group of Indians wouldn't enter the park until the next day, but their scouts were already camped by the Lower Geyser Basin.

The Nez Perce had repelled the army's predawn attack on their sleeping camp on the banks of the Big Hole River two weeks earlier. The Indians' chiefs wanted to avoid whites, but many of the young men were looking for a fight because the sneak attack under cover of darkness violated Nez Perce rules of war. Even worse, the soldiers had been ordered to shoot low into the teepees to kill Indians indiscriminately. The killing of women and children enraged the young warriors. Groups of a dozen or so young Indian men fanned out in all directions from the main body looking for horses to steal and whites to kill.

A twenty-one-year-old warrior named Yellow Wolf was one of the scouts in the park. In fact, he and his companions had already captured a prospector named John Shively. When they discovered Shively had been prospecting in the park for several weeks, they took him to their chiefs, who interrogated him. Shively agreed to guide the Indians through the park because he figured that was the only way he could save his life. He stayed with the Indians for thirteen days and led them to the northern edge of the park where they outmaneuvered the army and escaped to the Montana plains. Shively said he got away when the Indians weren't watching, but they said they let him go because they didn't need him anymore.

After Yellow Wolf and his companions delivered Shively to the chiefs, they prepared to camp near the Lower Geyser Basin. There they spotted a campfire half a mile away, but they decided to wait until morning to investigate because a boggy flat filled with boiling springs lay between them and the fire.

The blaze Yellow Wolf and his friends saw was a bonfire set by tourists from Radersburg, Montana, who were celebrating their last day in the park. A young wife named Emma Cowan and her companions had spent a week seeing the sights and were planning to head home the next day.

Emma couldn't sleep that night. She repeatedly came to the door of the tent she shared with her husband and peered out. Maybe she was just checking to make sure the bonfire hadn't spread. Maybe she was hoping to see Fountain Geyser erupt just one more time. But most likely, Emma was worried about running into the Nez Perce on the way home. She couldn't have known that Yellow Wolf and his companions had seen the bonfire. The next day the Indians would shoot Emma's husband and take her and her sister and brother captive.

While Emma fretted the night before her capture, Andy Weikert and his friends were camped near Tower Fall forty miles to the north. These ten young men from Helena, Montana, were on their way to see the grand geysers. Before they could get there, Nez Perce scouts attacked their camp and sent them scurrying into the wilderness. After the Indians left, Weikert and most of his friends—the ones who were still alive—headed back to McCartney's cabin. But two men went in the opposite direction deeper into the wilderness.

The Nez Perce held Emma Cowan and her siblings for two days, then released them. The trio made their way for three days through the roadless wilderness to McCartney's. By August 27, most of the Radersburg and Helena tourists had arrived at McCartney's, but others were still missing. And those still at the cabin weren't safe. Yellow Wolf and his enraged companions—and other groups of Nez Perce scouts—were closing in.

Most of the refugees caught rides back to Bozeman, but a few remained to wait for the stragglers, and Andy Weikert and Jim McCartney returned to the wilderness to find them. Weikert and McCartney buried the body of one of their friends at the campsite where the Nez Perce attacked the Helena Party, but they couldn't find two missing men. On their way back to Mammoth Hot Springs they ran into a band of eighteen Nez Perce scouts and fled in a hail of bullets. The Indians were on their way back to the main party of Nez Perce after attacking McCartney's cabin where they had killed a beloved music teacher and driven the Helena Party's amiable black cook into hiding.

A few days later the prospector John Shively escaped from the Indians and made his way to McCartney's and found the cabin empty. He didn't know that the body of a man the Indians had killed there lay buried nearby in a tin tub that soldiers had used for a temporary coffin.

CHAPTER 2

General Sherman's Trip

On June 24, 1877, General William Tecumseh Sherman sent a letter to Montana territorial governor Benjamin F. Potts that said he would start his "long promised visit" to Montana on July 4.[1] He wanted to see Yellowstone National Park, particularly the grand geysers of the Upper Geyser Basin.

General Sherman, whose famous March to the Sea was credited with breaking the will of the Confederacy and ending the Civil War, was commanding general of the entire U.S. Army in 1877. His official reason for the trip was to inspect forts the army needed to keep the peace on a hundred-thousand-square-mile stretch of plains in Montana and Dakota territories. He particularly wanted to see a new fort that was under construction at the confluence of the Bighorn and Little Bighorn rivers, an installation that would come to be called Fort Custer.

Just a year earlier, Sitting Bull and his coalition of Sioux and Northern Cheyenne had decimated the Seventh Cavalry under Colonel George Armstrong Custer at the Battle of the Little Bighorn near the site of the new fort. Sherman's soldiers were still rounding up errant Indians on the plains and forcing them onto reservations. Meanwhile, Sitting Bull and his Sioux warriors waited just across the Canadian border where they could launch an attack any time.

While Sherman had his small army scattered across the plains, farther west more Indian trouble was festering. Negotiations with several bands of Nez Perce along the Idaho-Washington border broke down and warfare erupted. The army was chasing six hundred Nez Perce on a flight that eventually would take them through Yellowstone National Park and across the plains to a surrender just forty-two miles from the Canadian border.

General Sherman began his trip by boarding a train in Saint Louis on July 4, 1877, and heading to Bismarck, Dakota Territory, via Chicago and Minneapolis. Bismarck was the end of the train line, so there he boarded the steamboat *Rosebud*, a sturdy sternwheeler with twin smokestacks. Sherman chose the *Rosebud* because it had a shallow draft and a powerful engine that could drive it up the swift waters of the Yellowstone River and its tributaries.

The *Rosebud* headed upriver from Bismarck to Fort Buford where the Yellowstone joins the Missouri. There she turned up the Yellowstone and steamed through the badlands to the mouth of the Powder River where Colonel Nelson Miles was supervising construction of a new fort and holding three hundred Indian prisoners. Sherman said when the soon-to-be-completed fort was finished the Indians wouldn't be able to return. The Northern Pacific Railroad and settlers would soon follow.

Sherman also noted that Fort Custer was an area where the Nez Perce often came from their homeland in Idaho to hunt buffalo "traversing the whole of Montana doing little or no damage." But he also noted that buffalo were scarce. Relentless hide hunters had slain bison by the millions to supply the demand for leather belts to run the nation's burgeoning factories. Sherman said, "We saw only four buffaloes (two of which we killed) in our course, whereas, 10 years ago we would have encountered a million."[2]

Sherman said, "I now regard the Sioux Indian problem, as a war question, as solved by the operations of General Miles last winter, and by the establishment of the two new posts on the Yellowstone now assured this summer. Boats come and go now where a year ago none would venture except with strong guards. Wood yards are being established to facilitate navigation, and the great mass of the hostiles have been forced to go to the agencies for food and protection, or have fled across the border into British territory."[3]

Sherman's little steamboat trembled as its engines labored against the stiff current while it continued to the Rosebud River. There it entered the Bighorn and made its way to the Little Bighorn where another fort was being built. Sherman noted that this fort was "in the very heart of the old Sioux country."

"With this post occupied by strong enterprising garrisons, these Sioux Indians can never regain this country, and they will be forced to remain at their agencies,"[4] he said. By "agencies," Sherman meant reservations, territories where Indians were forced to live under the jurisdiction of the U.S. Bureau of Indian Affairs.

Sherman's assessments applied not just to the Sioux. The disappearance of buffalo and the new forts on the Montana plains also doomed Nez Perce hopes of making a new life there.

A company of cavalry met Sherman at the mouth of the Bighorn to accompany him two hundred miles up the Yellowstone River and over the Bozeman Pass to their home base at Fort Ellis. After Sherman and his party made their way on an unimproved road for four days, they met a courier from Fort Ellis with a telegram ordering Sherman to hurry because a railroad strike had broken out back east. Sherman rushed to Fort Ellis, arriving on August 1 to discover the strike was over—but the Nez Perce had entered the Bitterroot Valley of Montana by bypassing army barricades in Lolo Canyon west of Missoula.

* * * *

Alarm spread through the territory when Montanans heard the Nez Perce were coming. Rural residents in the Bitterroot Valley abandoned the crops on their farms and headed to towns for safety. Others began to refurbish thirty-year-old trapper-era forts and to build new ones. Benjamin Potts, the territorial governor, asked the secretary of war for permission to recruit a militia along with arms and supplies, but he was turned down. However, Sherman told the governor volunteers could fight beside soldiers as long as they were under the command of regular army officers. He also said they would be compensated for their service.

On July 25 Captain Charles Rawn, who had been sent to Missoula just a month before to build a fort there, heard the Nez Perce were coming. He rushed to Lolo Canyon with thirty-five soldiers and fifty volunteers. At a point where the canyon was just two hundred yards wide, Rawn's men threw up a barricade of earth and logs. The Nez Perce were camped just two miles away.

The next day Captain Rawn met with Nez Perce chiefs, who asked permission to travel through the Bitterroot Valley and on to the buffalo country on the eastern Montana plains. Captain Rawn countered by demanding that the Indians surrender their arms. The chiefs refused and returned to their camp, but they agreed to meet again the next day.

That night, Potts arrived with volunteers, who swelled the number of armed men at the barricade to more than two hundred, enough to turn back an attack by the Nez Perce. Potts joined Captain Rawn the next morning, and they went out for another meeting with the chiefs. Again, the negotiations ended in stalemate, and the parties returned to their camps. Captain Rawn expected a battle the next day. Governor Potts and most of the volunteers left, apparently after the Indians promised them they would pass peacefully through the Bitterroot Valley.[5]

The next morning, while Captain Rawn's men nervously waited with their guns at the barricade, the Indians—six hundred men, women, and children, along with all their goods and 1,500 horses—climbed over the ridge on the north side of the canyon and passed around the soldiers. The Indians went on their way up the Bitterroot Valley singing and laughing. Apparently, they had made a deal with the civilian volunteers and thought they would be able to travel peacefully to the plains. The place where they bypassed the army became known as "Fort Fizzle."

When Sherman heard the Nez Perce had bypassed Captain Rawn's barricade and were on their way up the Bitterroot Valley, he reacted with aplomb. His officers, he thought, could handle the situation.

When the Indians left Idaho, they left the army's Department of Columbia under General Oliver Otis Howard and entered the Department of Dakota where Colonel John Gibbon commanded the Montana Division. Having two commanders in charge of stopping the Nez Perce complicated the chain of command and later resulted in lower-ranking officers dealing with conflicting orders.

"I do not propose to interfere," Sherman said, "but leave it to Gibbon and Howard to fight out this fight." He hoped infantry under Colonel Gibbon reinforced by volunteer militia could intercept the Nez Perce along the Big Hole River and drive them back against General Howard's six hundred men. Howard, Sherman said, would destroy the Indians, or more likely force them to scatter. Satisfied that his subordinates could subdue the Nez Perce, Sherman went ahead with his plan to visit Yellowstone National Park.

Sherman made his plan to tour the park while he was still in Washington, D.C., where he could review the reports and maps that had accumulated over the years. He decided to enter the park from the north up the Yellowstone, make his way down to the grand geysers, and return by the same route. It made for an efficient trip to bypass some sights going in and see them on the return trip.

With the Nez Perce traveling through Montana, Sherman wanted to minimize the impact of his trip on the soldiers and equipment available, so

Bottlers Ranch in the Paradise Valley North of Yellowstone Park is where several tourist parties that tangled with the Nez Perce in the summer of 1877 went to rest and recuperate.
NATIONAL PARK SERVICE PHOTO BY WILLIAM HENRY JACKSON, 1871

he took only four enlisted men with him. In addition to Sherman and the soldiers, the party consisted of Sherman's son, Tom, two colonels who had traveled with him from Washington as aides-de-camp, and a packer who served as a guide.

Despite his small entourage, Sherman dismissed the threat of Indians. "I do not suppose I run much risk," he said, "for we are all armed, and the hostile Indians rarely resort to the park, a poor region for game, and to their superstitious minds associated with hell by reason of its geysers and hot springs."[6] Just twenty days after Sherman left for the park, the Nez Perce began taking captives at the Lower Geyser Basin. With about a hundred warriors, the Indians could easily have overwhelmed Sherman's small party and taken the commanding general of the entire U.S. Army captive.

On August 4 Sherman and his men left Fort Ellis and made their way over Trail Creek Pass to the Paradise Valley of the Yellowstone. The next day they stopped at Bottlers Ranch, the halfway point between Fort Ellis and Mammoth Hot Springs. In 1867, Frederick Bottler settled across the river from where miners worked their claims in Emigrant Gulch and started the first permanent ranch in the Yellowstone Valley. Bottler soon had a thriving grain and cattle business and sold vegetables and dairy products to the miners. He supplemented his income as a Yellowstone Park guide and outfitter and ran an inn for tourists.

When Sherman reached the place where the Gardner River runs into the Yellowstone, he sent the wagons ahead to wait at Mammoth Hot Springs for his return. Then he headed east over the well-worn trail that led past Tower Fall, where a creek plunged straight down 132 feet from between rock pinnacles that gave it its name.

One of the few places where Sherman slowed his headlong rush to the grand geysers was the crossing of Mount Washburn. Rather than taking the most direct route, Sherman decided to climb to the pinnacle of the mountain. Obstructions on the trail forced him to walk the last thousand feet, but he thought the view from the top was worth the effort.

"From Mount Washburn," the general said, "is plainly seen, as on a map at one's feet, the whole of the National Park. . . . Any man standing on Mount Washburn feels as though the whole world were below him. The view is simply sublime."[7]

Sherman said the view from the top of Mount Washburn was "worth the labor of reaching it once, but not twice."

From the top of Mount Washburn, Sherman headed on through woods and meadows to the falls of the Yellowstone at the head of the Grand Canyon. With one of his aides, he found a point to view the Lower Falls. He described the canyon as "exquisite," but he didn't bother to see the Upper Falls.

Sherman decided not to make a side trip to see Yellowstone Lake. Instead, he rushed over Mary Mountain Pass—on the trail that the fleeing Nez Perce and the pursuing soldiers would follow later—to the Lower Geyser Basin, where he spent only two hours. Then he rushed on to what he called "the real object and aim of our visit,"[8] the grand geysers of the Upper Basin.

The group camped between Old Faithful and Castle geysers where they could see the Beehive and the Giantess. They spent a full day timing intervals between Old Faithful's eruptions and viewing several of the other geysers they located using the maps made by army topographers, Barlow and Heap, who mapped the park in 1871. After a packed twenty-seven-hour stay at the Upper Geyser Basin, they headed back to Fort Ellis.

On their return trip, the travelers consulted typographers' maps, and some of the men took side trips to sights they had bypassed on the inbound trip. Sherman's son, Tom, detoured to see the Upper Falls of the Yellowstone, but the general didn't bother. He did take a quick side trip to inspect the sole militarily significant point in the park, Baronett's Bridge, which was the only span across the Yellowstone River at that time, making it an important military facility. Just days after Sherman inspected the bridge, Nez Perce scouts set it aflame, an act that successfully slowed the army that was pursuing them.

When Sherman and his men arrived at Mammoth Hot Springs, they found their wagons and a comfortable camp waiting for them. After having lunch, the men toured the springs and availed themselves of the baths at McCartney's resort. McCartney had only two customers at his usually busy establishment. In previous years there were dozens of tourists near McCartney at Mammoth Hot Springs, but apparently the Nez Perce troubles kept them away in the summer of 1877, although miners continued to pass through on their way to the Clarks Fork Mines near the northeast corner of the park.

Sherman's party left Mammoth Hot Springs for Fort Ellis on the afternoon of August 16. Late in the day they encountered two men who told them that the Nez Perce had repelled Colonel Gibbon's forces at the Big Hole and fled. Colonel Gibbon had been wounded, and several officers and many men were killed. The report disturbed Sherman's aide-de-camp Colonel Poe, who said, "The meager details indicated disaster."[9] As darkness fell the worried men made camp.

The next day they broke camp early and rushed ahead to get more news about the Big Hole Battle.

At Henderson's Ranch about seven miles north of the park, they found a packet of newspapers and telegrams that provided details of the battle. The newspaper packet doubtless included the August 11 issue of the Helena *Daily Herald* with the headlines "A Bloody Battle" and "The Command Reported to Have Lost One Half in Killed and Wounded." Sherman and his companions were relieved to learn that Colonel Gibbon had not been critically injured. They rushed back to Fort Ellis, stopping just a few minutes on Trail Creek Pass to trade information with tourists who were heading to the park. These tourists were members of the Helena Party, two of whom Nez Perce scouts killed a few days later.

Sherman and his party forced their horses thirty-four miles more and got to Fort Ellis at two in the afternoon. There the general could review official army reports and newspaper accounts of the Big Hole Battle. The information he saw showed that when it became clear the Nez Perce were headed to Montana, Colonel John Gibbon received orders telling him to disarm, dismount, and capture them. Colonel Gibbon ordered all troops that could be spared from posts under his command to convene at Fort Missoula, which was 150 miles from his home base at Fort Shaw in central Montana. Other men came from Fort Ellis, 240 miles away, and Camp Baker near White Sulphur Springs, 190 miles from Missoula.

On August 4, Colonel Gibbon's combined forces, fifteen officers and 146 enlisted men, left Fort Missoula and camped twenty-five miles away. There they were joined by forty-five civilian volunteers, bringing the colonel's force to more than two hundred. The combined soldiers and volunteers outnumbered Nez Perce men of fighting age by more than two to one.

The army traveled forty-five miles on the second day, and on the third day their scouts found the Indians' camp about a hundred miles from Fort Missoula. The Nez Perce had made a leisurely trip up the Bitterroot Valley and crossed into the drainage of the Big Hole River. There they stopped to rest at a site where they traditionally camped on their annual buffalo hunting trips to Montana. They planned to rest, graze their horses, and harvest new teepee poles after their battles with General Howard's army and their arduous flight. Their chiefs decided not to post guards because they thought that would be an affront to the Montana settlers to whom they had promised to travel peacefully past to the buffalo country on the plains.

When Colonel Gibbon heard from his scouts that the Indians had been found, he immediately began plans for an attack. He had his men stop and have a cold dinner of salt pork and hardtack because he feared the Indians might see campfires. At 11 p.m. on August 8, Colonel Gibbon ordered his underfed and travel-weary men forward. By 2 a.m. they were in position on the North Fork of the Big Hole River across from the sleeping Indians' camp. They had orders to shoot as soon as they saw movement.

A lone Indian rode out at dawn, apparently to check on his horses, and several soldiers gunned him down. The troops then attacked the sleeping village, and the fighting devolved into close combat. When the soldiers began shooting into teepees and setting them afire, they discovered they weren't fighting just Indian men. Indian women picked up guns and shot soldiers dead.

At first the Indians scattered, but Nez Perce chiefs rallied them and they began a counterattack, and Colonel Gibbon was shot in the leg. Seeing his men being decimated, the colonel ordered a retreat back across the river to a nearby grove of trees. The soldiers fought their way to the timber and dug trenches with their trowel bayonets.

While the Nez Perce men battled the army, their women hastily packed their belongings, buried their dead in shallow graves, and rounded up their horses. The next day, the Indians left twenty or thirty riflemen armed with lever-action repeating rifles to keep more than 150 soldiers and volunteers pinned down with their single-shot breach loaders. That night the sharp-shooters left to join the fleeing tribe.

The battle was costly to both sides. Twenty-nine of Colonel Gibbon's men were killed. Estimates of Nez Perce dead range between seventy and ninety, about two-thirds of them women and children. The battle ended the Indians' hopes of traveling peacefully to the Montana plains. While Nez Perce leaders still wanted to avoid conflict, many young Indian men were bent on vengeance and began attacking ranches, stealing horses, and killing white men.

After the battle, Colonel Gibbon spent several days supervising the burial of his dead men and tending the wounds of the living. He finally arrived in Deer Lodge on August 14, where there was a hospital to treat his wounds and those of his men. Deer Lodge also had a telegraph office, from which Colonel Gibbon sent orders to Fort Ellis for officers there to hire civilian scouts to find out if the Nez Perce were headed toward settlements in the Gallatin Valley or would detour through Yellowstone Park.

Although Colonel Gibbon had failed to capture the Nez Perce, General Sherman still trusted his subordinates to subdue them. After a short rest at Fort Ellis, Sherman went to the Montana territorial capital in Helena where his party was feted with elaborate balls, and then he continued his tour of northwest forts. General Sherman got his cherished visit to Yellowstone's grand geysers, but not the resolution to the Nez Perce problem he had hoped for. In two weeks those Indians would see the geysers themselves.

CHAPTER 3

Radersburg to Geyserland

The hot, dry weather in the summer of 1877 brought hordes of Rocky Mountain locusts to the upper Missouri River Valley.[1] The grasshoppers swarmed so thickly that twenty-two-year-old Emma Cowan had to seal up every crack in her house in Radersburg to keep them out. All she could do was to wait in the sweltering heat for her husband, George, to come home, and George was busy with his job as Jefferson County attorney. Emma was still childless after nearly two years of marriage, and keeping house for just two people must have been boring. She described her situation as "almost unbearable." It's no wonder that when her brother arrived from Helena and announced he was mounting an expedition to Yellowstone Park, she jumped at the chance to join it.

But bugs, heat, and boredom weren't the only reasons Emma wanted to visit the park. A trip to geyserland would fulfill a dream she had nurtured for more than a decade. Emma came to Montana in a covered wagon during the gold rush of 1864. She recalled that trip fondly: "I enjoyed beyond measure the gypsy style of travel, journeying toward the setting sun, expecting in all probability to find a pot of gold at the end of the rainbow's point. For the land of gold was the objective place."[2]

Emma and her family crossed the plains without encountering Indians, a fact that bothered her when she was a little girl. She was envious of the adventures her friends told about Indian encounters. But Emma admitted, "We were very fortunate for we were poorly equipped for defense."[3] Her father had little fear of Indians and didn't even carry a gun.

Emma's family settled in the gold rush town of Virginia City where her father ran a butcher shop. To supply ravenous miners there who wouldn't take time from searching for gold to find food, he purchased beef from local ranchers, wild game from professional hunters, and fish from a supplier who harvested them from Henrys Lake, an eight-square-mile body of water located seventy miles south of Virginia City and twenty-five miles west of

Emma Cowan was taken captive by the Nez Perce on August 24, 1877.
She was released two days later and fled northward across the park with her
brother and sister.

MONTANA HISTORICAL SOCIETY PHOTO

Yellowstone's grand geysers. The fisherman was Gilman Sawtell, a blue-eyed blond who came West after serving as a Union soldier in the Civil War. At first Sawtell prospected for gold, but he soon gave that up and began homesteading at Henrys Lake. Nobody knows when Sawtell began visiting the area that became Yellowstone Park, but he was telling stories about geysers by the mid-1860s.

One day when Emma was living in Virginia City, her father brought Sawtell home from the butcher shop to meet his family. Sawtell regaled Emma and her siblings with stories about things he had seen. Emma said, "My fairy books could not equal such wonderful tales. Fountains of boiling water, crystal clear, thrown hundreds of feet into the air, only to fall back into pools of their own forming; pools of water in whose limpid depths tints of various rainbows were reflected; mounds and terraces of gaily colored sand."[4] Emma and her family thought Sawtell's stories were just fantasies, but she said, "As I grew older and found truth in the statements, the desire to someday visit this land was ever present."[5]

Emma first visited Yellowstone Park in 1873 with her parents, but she didn't see geyserland. Instead, the Cowans went up the rugged new road through Yankee Jim Canyon to Mammoth Hot Springs. Although the park was just a year old when Emma and her family first visited there, Mammoth Hot Springs had already become a tourist destination. Emma said, "We found an acquaintance or two, a number of strangers, a small hotel and a bath house."[6]

Emma and her family stayed at Mammoth Hot Springs for two weeks. There they could climb the white terraces and view the multicolored pools, soak in hot baths, and make souvenirs by leaving items in pools where mineral waters encrusted them with a pure, white coat. They could have hired guides to take them to the Grand Canyon of the Yellowstone, the falls, and, most important, the grand geysers. But that would have required an arduous seventy-five-mile trip on horseback across the roadless wilderness, so they decided against it.

Several parties returned from geyserland during Emma's stay at Mammoth in 1873, and their accounts intrigued her. "You must see them for yourself,"[7] they told her. Emma's interest was piqued, so when she got home she learned everything she could about geysers from magazines, newspapers, and people's accounts. Emma got her chance to visit geyserland in 1877 when her twenty-seven-year-old brother, Frank Carpenter, mounted an expedition to the park.

When Frank started planning his trip, he thought he would go with just one companion, Al Oldham, another young Helena man. Frank's plan was typical for the time: a couple of young men on horseback with a single pack animal. They couldn't carry enough food for their six-week trip, so they planned to live off the land. When they camped by a stream they could usually catch enough fish for a meal in half an hour. As they traveled along, they might shoot a sage grouse or an antelope beside the road. If they took a side trip for hunting, they might even bag a deer or an elk.

In addition to the camaraderie of close friends, the fun of hunting and fishing and the wonder of seeing Yellowstone's sights, Frank planned to write a book about his adventures. He kept a journal detailing his trip until the day the Nez Perce captured him and his sisters and scattered his notes on the ground.

While Frank and Al Oldham were buying horses and assembling equipment for their trip, they told another Helena friend, A. J. Arnold, about it and he wanted to join them. On July 2, 1877, the three young men left for Frank's father's ranch forty-five miles south of Helena near Radersburg.

When Frank got to Radersburg and told his twenty-two-year-old married sister, Emma Cowan, that he was going to the park, she insisted on joining him. Because she didn't want to be the only female on the trip, she also talked her mother into letting her thirteen-year-old sister, Ida, come along. Emma explained, "She would be so much company for me."[8]

The addition of women meant the expedition could no longer plan to sleep outside and live off the land. They now needed a wagon for tents and supplies and a carriage for the ladies. Other people from Radersburg joined the expedition, and Emma's husband, George, hired a cook and a driver for the supply wagon. When what became known as the "Radersburg Party" left on August 5, it included nine people: Emma Cowan, her husband, George, and her sister, Ida; Emma's brother Frank Carpenter and three of his friends, A. J. Arnold, J. A. Oldham, and William Dingee; the cook, Charles Mann; and a young man to drive the supply wagon, Henry Meyers of Radersburg.

The group's wagons and riders spread out as they traveled through the settled areas along the upper Missouri River Valley. George drove fleet carriage horses that pulled the comfortable double-seated buggy carrying

MRS. COWAN

GEO. F. COWAN

CHIEF JOSEPH NEZ PERCE

IDA CARPENTER

FRANK CARPENTER

This montage shows members of the Radersburg Party around a photo of Chief Joseph. Upper left, Emma Cowan. Upper right, George Cowan. Lower left, Ida Carpenter. Lower right, Frank Carpenter.

Emma, Ida, and George's beloved dog, Dido. Frank and his friends ranged far and wide on horseback. Young Henry Meyers drove the supply wagon that was pulled by ponderous draft horses and lumbered slowly behind the others, often falling far behind.

Emma said the party was well equipped with "provisions, tents, guns, and last, but not least, musical instruments."[9] The group anticipated many jolly evenings singing around the campfire with Al Oldham on the violin, Frank on guitar, and the others singing and dancing.

The group had four extra saddle horses so the carriage riders could take off-road excursions whenever they felt like it. One of those horses was Emma's pony, a gift from her father that she named "Bird, because she was trim and fleet."[10]

The first afternoon while Frank and his friends rode along a ridge twenty miles south of Radersburg, they spied three pronghorn antelope lying in the road about three hundred yards ahead. As the riders came near, the antelope jumped to their feet and stared at the passersby with their big, black eyes. Here was meat for the larder—and sport for the young men.

The riders dismounted and parleyed to determine who would get the honor of spilling "first blood," a common contest of the time. One of the men aimed his rifle and fired. The antelope looked surprised. Another marksman stepped forward, took a long aim, and fired. Only then did the antelope deign to move. After the men fired a half dozen more shots, the animals paused and looked back as if to acknowledge the attention they had received. Then they dashed away with their white rumps bobbing up and down. The nimrods weren't humbled by their lack of success. Instead of blaming their marksmanship, they jovially blamed their guns.

The travelers headed across the bench west of the Missouri River. By late afternoon the band of willows and cottonwood groves that lined the edge of the river widened. There the Gallatin River flowed into the combined Madison and Jefferson rivers, marking the official head of the Missouri. The travelers stayed on the open bench past the point where the Madison and Jefferson joined and continued south. They traveled two miles farther up the Jefferson and found a spot to camp.

While the men set up camp, Emma and Ida decided to pay their respects at a nearby ranch house. Such a social call was not just acceptable; it would have been rude for ladies to come so close and not say hello, even to strangers.

But the ranch house residents weren't strangers. Emma and Ida were delighted to discover that they were friends from Radersburg who had recently married and moved to the ranch. The ranchers invited Emma and Ida to have supper with them and asked the rest of the party to spend the evening later.

With the women gone, the men began preparing their supper. Soon the cook greeted them with the traditional call to eat—"grub pile."

Billy Dingee, who was always eager to eat, announced that he expected to lose twenty pounds on the trip. His prediction came true, but not in the way he expected. He proceeded to wolf down so much food that no one was surprised later when he reported that he wasn't feeling well. He volunteered to stay at the camp and wash dishes while the others went to the festivities at the ranch.

At eleven that night, the revelers—except for Emma and Ida who decided to spend the night at their friends' house—returned to find Dingee still sick. Frank said he looked like he was "trying to skin a cat through his mouth."[11] But by daybreak, Dingee had recovered his ravenous appetite and yelled "grub pile" when breakfast was ready.

The travelers made their way up the Jefferson River and crossed at a toll bridge. By nightfall, they had gone more than thirty miles and were approaching Sterling, a mining town tucked in the eastern edge of the Tobacco Root Mountains. The baggage wagon had fallen far behind, so Frank and his friends had to wait for it. George decided to take Emma and Ida to the hotel in town for supper. There several townspeople advised them to turn back because of "Indian trouble." Newspapers that would have come to Sterling from Helena and Bozeman via stagecoach reported that the Nez Perce had bypassed barricades the army had put up to stop them in Lolo Canyon and were making their way up the Bitterroot Valley. Newspaper coverage of the Indian situation was mixed.[12] Some stories noted that the Nez Perce said they just wanted to travel peacefully to the buffalo country in eastern Montana, something they had done many times in previous years. But other stories reported that ranch families all along the route the Nez Perce normally traveled were rushing to take shelter in towns.

Emma said she thought the news was nothing but an old-time Indian scare like those her father laughed about when she was a little girl. "When the next morning came bright and beautiful," she said, "we decided to go on our way."[13]

While the Cowans and Ida enjoyed their meal at the hotel in Sterling, the Nez Perce were setting up camp along the banks of the Big Hole River 130 miles west of them. The Indians had left General Howard and his troops behind in Idaho, skirted a barricade thrown up by soldiers and volunteers, negotiated a truce with Montana settlers, and made their way peacefully up the Bitterroot Valley. They thought they had left the war behind, so they settled in at their traditional campsite where they could let their tired livestock graze on the lush grass and harvest new lodge poles to replace those abandoned or worn out during their hasty retreat. The chief leading the Nez Perce then, Looking Glass, decided not to post sentries because he thought that would be an affront to the settlers who had promised the Indians safe passage to the buffalo country. The decision proved fatal when the army attacked their sleeping camp two days later, killing more than seventy people, most of them women and children.

After spending the night at Sterling, the Radersburg Party headed south through the Madison River Valley. The Spanish Peaks on the east side of the valley and the Tobacco Root Mountains to the west carved a jagged skyline of igneous rock.

By noon the group had traveled twenty miles to the town of Ennis, where George found out that they would be able to borrow fishing equipment—boats, spears, skeins, and tackle of all kinds—at Gilman Sawtell's ranch at Henrys Lake. But Sawtell himself was helping a nearby rancher put up hay and wouldn't be at the lake. Emma was disappointed by the news because she remembered Sawtell as the man who had told her marvelous tales of Yellowstone Park when she was a girl in Virginia City. One of the men rode to the ranch where Sawtell was working and borrowed a key to the buildings at Henrys Lake, but Emma still wished she could have heard him tell his stories again.

South of Ennis the travelers passed the last ranch and headed into the unsettled wilderness. They left the Spanish Peaks behind, but the Madison Mountain Range still rose dramatically from the valley floor to the east. The less imposing Gravelly Range bound the west. The Madison River ambled down the valley with a green stripe of meadows and cottonwood groves along its banks. Every ten miles or so a clear mountain stream tumbled out of the mountains and cut across the dry benches, making a green path of pines, cottonwoods, and verdure.

The carriage and the supply wagon traveled easily on the road Gilman Sawtell built between Henrys Lake and Virginia City. Frank and his friends foraged far and wide across the valley. Hunting was good, and the men bagged antelope and sage hens for their evening meals. George even shot two bald eagles, just for sport. Back then such wanton killing for fun seemed normal. People apparently believed the land would renew itself and provide an endless supply of wildlife.

The only excitement occurred when the men spied what they thought might be Indian ponies in the distance. Even if the Nez Perce hadn't been on the move, seeing Indians in the Madison Valley would not have been a surprise. The area was known as an "Indian runway" where numerous tribes from the south and west passed through on their way to the buffalo country on the plains of Montana. Frank and Dingee rode ahead to check out the animals they had seen. When they climbed a hill where they could see the objects just two miles away, they discovered a herd of grazing cattle.

After three days, the travelers came to the mouth of the Madison Canyon where the river flowed between two mountains of rock hundreds of feet high. The shortest route to the Yellowstone geysers was through that canyon, but huge boulders and thick timber blocked the way. Men on horseback could make it through on game trails, but there was no wagon road.[14] Instead of heading through the canyon, the travelers went southward over the gentle Raynolds Pass. That was a small sacrifice because the detour meant they could stop for rest and recreation at Henrys Lake.

From the summit of Raynolds Pass, the travelers could see the three Teton peaks carving a jagged line across they skyline far to the south. Even in August, patches of snow dotted the soaring pinnacles.

Coveys of grouse scurried around the sagebrush near the road, but the travelers didn't stop to hunt. They were hurrying to Henrys Lake, a well-known paradise for sportsmen. The five-mile-long lake teemed with fish, ducks, swans, and pelicans. Antelope and grouse populated the nearby hillsides, and deer and elk roamed the mountains. Equally important, there was lush grass on the lakeshore where travel-weary horses could graze and rejuvenate.

After a few miles, the gleaming waters of the lake came into view. Marshes and willow thickets that provided a haven for waterfowl surrounded most of the lakeshore. But the travelers found a spot of solid ground near

Sawtell's compound. After settling at Henrys Lake a decade before, Sawtell built a veritable village of sturdy log buildings including a residence, a blacksmith shop, a stable, a shed for storing hides and game, and an ice house for keeping fish cold.[15] Two boats were moored on a spring-fed stream that passed through the marsh and provided access to the lake.

Frank and his friends promptly commandeered a boat and took Ida out to explore the verdant islands that floated on the lake about half a mile from shore. As they returned, the girl tossed a line over the stern of the boat to troll for fish. She soon hooked a large trout and pulled it aboard. She caught three more fish before the sailors reached shore.

After the supply wagon arrived, the travelers made camp about three hundred yards from the lake. After sunset, moonlight shimmered across the calm lake.

In his journal, Frank reported, "After supper the guitar and violin were brought out and we passed a jolly evening. Mr. Dingee performed some astonishing feats of dance in which he demonstrated a 'double shuffle' and 'pigeon wing,' and Al Oldham recited poetry. At 11, Dingee declared the circus closed."[16]

The travelers went to sleep while the wild birds kept up a chorus of discordant sounds. Each kind of bird—ducks, pelicans, and cranes—screamed out as if trying to outdo the others. Above all came the sweet, strong, melodious whistle of the swans.

The travelers decided to devote the next day to exploring. George and Emma took the horses and rode into the nearby mountains. They said they were going to hunt for big game, deer, or even elk. But maybe they just wanted some private time together. The newlyweds planned to spend their second wedding anniversary in Yellowstone Park, and they had been sharing their tent with Ida for more than a week.

Meyers and Mann took the small boat and rowed out to find a good spot where Mann could sketch the scenery. The other men decided to take the large boat all the way across the lake to the spot where the Henrys Fork of the Snake River runs out of Henrys Lake. They loaded the boat with guns, fishing tackle, and food for a picnic. They planned to spend the whole day fishing, hunting, and cavorting about.

With their usual bravado, Dingee and Arnold proclaimed themselves "Old Salts" and declared Frank and Oldham were nothing but "land lubbers."

As the men rowed down the stream that led from Sawtell's compound to the lake, Dingee laced the conversation with sailor talk—"shiver me timbers" and "all hands on deck."

Once the crew got out on the lake, Dingee rigged a makeshift mast, hoisted a sail, and ordered everybody to "ship oars." The boat coasted to a stop, and the sail flapped in the light breeze. Following an old sailor's superstition, Dingee stabbed his jackknife into the mast and swore. When that failed to summon an adequate wind, the crew pulled down the sail and started to row.

The men rowed for several miles across the lake, stopping now and then to shoot at passing swans. When they had almost reached their destination, a stiff breeze came up and Dingee ordered the crew to "heist" the sail. After hours of rowing, the compliant crew eagerly obeyed. The wind filled the unfurled sail and jerked the boat over, almost capsizing it. But the crew's quick action kept the craft upright, and soon they were scooting across the lake.

As they approached the south end of the lake, the sailors spotted a family of swans. The parents flew away, leaving six cygnets gliding across the water. The men gleefully shot five of the young birds and captured the sixth.

The sailors went ashore where the Henrys Fork flowed out of the lake and hiked downstream looking for good fishing holes and taking an occasional pot shot at passing game. Toward evening, they returned to the boat and found a stiff breeze blowing from the north where the camp was. The men manned the oars and began rowing along the shore.

When they passed some ripe, black currants, the ever-ravenous Dingee declared they must stop and pick a few. Frank reported, "We picked an immense quantity; at least this is the inference from Dingee's assertion that 'he had enough.'"[17]

While the men gorged themselves on currants, the wind picked up. It still blew in the wrong direction, so when they returned to the boat rowing was even harder. Soon, the tired rowers acquiesced to Dingee's confident assertion that he could tack upwind. He said, "Anybody could do it who knew how."[18]

Dingee rigged the sail and took the helm. Frank declared, "We stood in awe of his superior knowledge and gazed in silent admiration upon the man as he set the sail."[19]

Dingee's first tack brought the sailors back to the mouth of the river and left the boat a third full of water.

Dingee explained that his knowledge of saltwater sailing apparently didn't apply on a freshwater lake. The men took down the sail and began the hard work of rowing against the wind. Darkness began to fall.

Back at Sawtell's compound, George and Emma returned from hunting after a long day in the saddle. They hadn't seen a single deer or elk or even a track. They were surprised to find the camp deserted.

Emma later recalled, "The day, which had been lovely, changed with the setting sun. Great banks of clouds came scurrying across the sky. The sighing of the wind through the pines brought the thought of storms, the darkness was coming rapidly and the day ended drearily."[20]

Fearing that some accident had befallen the sailors, Emma and George built a huge bonfire to serve as a beacon in the coming darkness. Finally, Emma heard a faint "hello" traveling across the water. It took another half hour of hard rowing, but at last, the sailors reached shore, tired but jolly. After a good supper, the travelers gathered around the campfire to sing and tell stories.

The next day, August 12, was Sunday, the day of rest, so the travelers mostly lolled around camp. Frank and his friends used the time to skin the swans they killed the day before. They wanted to save the valuable down.[21]

The men took George for a quick trip on the lake, and he shot a giant swan with an eight-foot wingspan. Frank captured a young swan and brought it back to camp. Despite the efforts of George's dog, Dido, to keep the cygnet in line, the young swan made a pest of itself. Frank agreed to return it to the lake, but only after his companions agreed to help him capture another one when they returned.

While scouting Sawtell's compound, Frank and his friends found what they thought was a hay shed that contained fish spears, eight-foot poles with forged iron points.

That night they set a hundred pine knots ablaze in the prow of one of the boats. The glare attracted giant schools of fish, and the men speared thirty-five of them in half an hour.

Emma said, "Great schools of fish, attracted by the glare of light from a hundred blazing pine knots gathered about the prow of the boat."

Frank Carpenter said, "We had a pleasant time for a half hour, spearing in that time some thirty-five salmon trout."[22]

A strong wind came up, cutting the fishing expedition short. When the men returned the spears to the building where they found them, they decided to spend the night there. After they lay down, Frank commented that he thought the floor where they slept seemed rather hard and cold. After a fitful night, the men discovered they had taken possession of Sawtell's ice house and slept on a sheet of ice covered by a layer of sawdust.

On Monday, August 13, the Radersburg Party left Henrys Lake and headed over Targhee Pass to geyserland. The same day, another party of tourists, called the Helena Party, began their ill-fated Yellowstone vacation. Also that day, young Nez Perce braves, who were enraged by the army's sneak attack on their sleeping camp at the Big Hole, ignored their chiefs' admonitions to remain calm and began killing settlers at Horse Prairie ninety miles west of Henrys Lake.

Targhee Pass was gentle, and the Radersburg Party moved at a leisurely pace over Sawtell's new road. The men rode ahead of the wagons, seeing the sights and scouting the way. It was an easy climb with the road going through meadows and evergreen forests.

As the wagons approached a thick stand of timber, Emma and Ida heard galloping horses. Then riders dashed into view and breathlessly warned: "Indians ahead." The ladies were used to the men's antics, so their Indian scare joke failed. But everybody believed the men when they said there was no water ahead for ten miles, and the party turned back to a spot with a welcoming spring and made camp for the night.

Soon Dingee was yelling "grub pile" and the travelers dug into an early supper. Al Oldham looked for a comfortable spot and sat on hot, stewed peaches. Frank Carpenter said, "He sprang to his feet, dropped his plate, grasped the seat of his breeches with both hands, looked heavenward, and paid emphatic tribute to his Maker by one single ejaculation."[23] The injury restricted Oldham's movement for the remainder of the journey.

When the diners looked down the hill, they saw a pair of pack animals approaching. The tourists thought the animals must be from General William Tecumseh Sherman's party. The famous Civil War hero was commanding general of the army, so everybody knew he was visiting Yellowstone Park then. But the men the Radersburg Party met that day weren't General

Sherman's, although they had seen the Civil War hero two days before. They were prospectors named Hicks and Wood. The prospectors recounted meeting the famous general and warned that downed timber blocked the route ahead to the geysers. Hicks and Wood then returned to their camp.

The next day when Frank went to round up the Radersburg Party's horses, he passed the prospectors' camp, and they offered him a hearty greeting, "So long, good luck to you." Then the prospectors headed down the Madison River straight into the area where young Nez Perce scouts were taking revenge on any white man they could find. Hicks and Wood were never seen again.

The Radersburg Party made their way up the Madison River with the men riding ahead to find Sawtell's new road, which was often hard to see. Finally the travelers came to the spot Hicks and Wood had warned about where dead trees had toppled in all directions, creating a tangle that blocked the road. The men took out their axes and chopped their way through the fallen timber for more than a mile. After coming into open country, the travelers proceeded for another mile to a fork in the river. There they fixed a huge meal to feed the men who were ravenous for their hard work and camped for the night.

The next day they entered the upper Madison Canyon where the roadway was crowded between rushing clear water and giant gray walls of igneous rock. In places, thick stands of timber blocked the way, forcing the travelers to ford the river. But the spring snowmelt was over so the water was shallow, and the river's gravel bottom was solid. That was good because they crossed the river seven times in only six miles.

They emerged from the canyon and came to the spot where the Gibbon and Firehole rivers join to form the Madison. This was the last place on their route where fishing was good. There were no fish in the Firehole River further on. Early travelers assumed the fishless river was due to hot waters from geysers and springs, but that was wrong. Actually, waterfalls and cascades formed by massive lava flows millions of years before kept fish from migrating upstream after Ice Age glaciers melted ten thousand years ago.[24]

After stocking up on fish, the travelers crossed the Gibbon and left the stream climbing the divide that separates it from the Madison. The road was good, and they found wild strawberry and raspberry on its borders. About 3 o'clock they came out of the forest and crested a hill, and a wide, swampy meadow spread before them. In the distance they saw dozens of columns of steam that contrasted sharply with the pine forest green hills beyond. At the bottom of some of the steam columns, they saw boiling water thrusting skyward. They had arrived in geyserland.

CHAPTER 4

Scouts Search for the Nez Perce

After repelling the army at the Big Hole Battle, the Nez Perce left a small group of warriors to keep their attackers pinned down. Then the Indians hurriedly buried their dead and headed south carrying their wounded on travois. They buried people who died along the way at overnight campsites. The seriously wounded and those too old and feeble to keep up stayed behind to die or be dispatched by pursuers rather than slow down the tribe's march.

One of General Howard's civilian scouts told of coming upon an old man sitting on a buffalo robe with only a bottle of water. The helpless old man pointed a finger at his head and pulled an imaginary trigger to indicate that he wanted the scout to put him out of his misery. The scout refused but said he heard a gunshot after he rode away. He figured one of the Bannock Indians with General Howard had dispatched the old man.[1]

When the Indians camped at the Big Hole, Looking Glass, the chief who was in charge at the time, kept them from posting a rear guard, although some of his men wanted him to. He said the Nez Perce were fighting the small army detachment from Fort Missoula that wouldn't be foolish enough to attack them.[2] The surprise attack at the Big Hole left the Nez Perce with no hope that whites would allow them to pass peacefully through Montana.

Because there were civilian volunteers with the army units that attacked at the Big Hole, the Nez Perce chiefs couldn't convince young warriors that they should fight only soldiers. The problem of avoiding attacks on white setters was exacerbated by the need to send out scouts to avoid another surprise attack.

After the attack at the Big Hole, young Nez Perce men began ranging for twenty or thirty miles in all directions from the main group that included women, children, and old men. The scouts didn't just watch for soldiers. They hunted for food and looked for campsites that would provide fresh water, firewood, and grazing for their herd of 1,500 horses and cattle. They also rounded up all the horses they could find, not only to supplement their own

29

herd but also to deprive the army of fresh mounts. These efforts to take horses frequently resulted in gun battles and killing of whites.

News that the Nez Perce were on the move sent waves of terror ahead of them. At the mining town of Bannack fifty miles south of the Big Hole battlefield, residents and people from nearby ranches barricaded themselves in a new brick courthouse. They covered the courthouse windows with mattresses, brought in a barrel of water, and fortified a route to a nearby well.[3]

After the Big Hole Battle, Colonel John Gibbon had to wait several days at the battlefield because the Indians had taken his horses. When rescue wagons finally arrived to carry the wounded, Gibbon's army trudged northeast seventy-five miles to Deer Lodge where there was a hospital and a telegraph office.

Gibbon's effort to capture the Nez Perce at the Big Hole had failed, and the army didn't know where the Indians were going. At first, there was speculation that the Nez Perce might be returning to their homeland because they had crossed back into Idaho. But they soon headed east again toward the buffalo country on the Montana plains by turning up the Henrys Fork of the Snake River toward Henrys Lake. From Henrys Lake, the Nez Perce could go either over Targhee Pass into Yellowstone Park or down the Madison River Valley toward the settlements near Bozeman. The army needed to know if they had to deploy troops to protect civilians in the valley or if they should try to contain the Indians in the park.

When finally Gibbon got to Deer Lodge on August 13, 1877, he sent a telegram to Fort Ellis directing officers there to hire experienced scouts to find out where the Indians were headed. He might even have known that the perfect candidates were already in Bozeman.

One of them was George Herendeen, who had accompanied General William Tecumseh Sherman from the incipient Fort Custer to Fort Ellis near Bozeman. Herendeen had been a scout with Custer's ill-fated Seventh Cavalry when it was wiped out just one year before on June 25, 1876, at the Battle of the Little Bighorn.

Herendeen survived Custer's Last Stand because he was assigned to the battalion commanded by Major Marcus Reno, which didn't participate in the battle. Herendeen earned lasting fame by providing the first eyewitness account of Custer's Last Stand. After the battle he rushed nearly four hundred miles to the telegraph office in Bismarck, Dakota Territory, where he

Fort Ellis located west of Bozeman, Montana, was the launching point of several army efforts to find the Nez Perce and contain them in Yellowstone Park.
NATIONAL PARK SERVICE PHOTO BY WILLIAM HENRY JACKSON, 1871

provided the first written description of the battle. Herendeen's account was reprinted in newspapers across the nation.[4]

Another experienced Indian fighter, Jack Bean, lived near Bozeman. Bean had been in charge of the pack train under Colonel John Gibbon in the Montana Column, which was supposed to help Custer.[5] The Montana Column was a combined unit of infantry and cavalry that went out from Fort Ellis and Fort Shaw to help force the recalcitrant Sioux and Cheyenne onto reservations. But Custer thought the Indians had discovered his force and rushed the attack without waiting for Gibbon and his men. The Montana Column arrived at the battlefield two days later. Bean was among the men who found the mutilated bodies of Custer and his men.

In a reminiscence, Bean said he told the officer who recruited him to find the Nez Perce: "I was getting tired of Indian warfare but told him that I would go if George Herendeen would go with me."[6]

"That settles it,"[7] the officer replied. Herendeen had already agreed to go—but only if Bean would.

31

Yellowstone guide Jack Bean, who along with fellow Indian fighter George Herendeen, was hired by the army to find out where the Nez Perce were headed after the Big Hole Battle.

GALLATIN HISTORY MUSEUM PHOTO

The officer was eager for the scouts to leave so he could send a message to Colonel Gibbon saying they were on their way before the telegraph office closed at 7 p.m. While Herendeen and Bean went to a nearby ranch to fetch their horses, the officer went to Fort Ellis to get rations for them.

When the men arrived at the Gallatin River about twelve miles west of Bozeman, they stopped to brew coffee and eat, but they discovered the rations the army provided were infested. Bean said they broke their hardtack, shook off the bugs, and ate. Then they reloaded their packhorse and rode through the night.

By sunrise, Bean and Herendeen had crossed over the rolling hills that divided the Gallatin and Madison river valleys. They talked with settlers there who feared the Nez Perce might be coming their way and had sent out scouts to watch for the Indians.

Herendeen and Bean rode across the dry benches of the Madison Valley all day and into the night. When they finally stopped to sleep, they took a good look around. Bean said, "As we saw signal fires that night on the high mountains, we were quite sure the Indians would come up the Snake River to Henrys Lake."[8]

The next morning, Bean and Herendeen encountered the scouts that the Madison Valley settlers had told them about. The Madison scouts had also seen the signal fires but thought lightning had caused them. Bean scoffed and pointed out that it had been a clear night. The trio then conceded that the fires must have been Nez Perce signals and agreed to come with Herendeen and Bean to Henrys Lake.

At the lake, the group waited all day for the Indians to arrive but saw nothing. As the full moon rose, Bean climbed to the top of an old log house with his field glasses. The others asked when he was going to bed, but he told them he had a hunch he should watch a little longer.

Soon he saw a fire flickering about a mile away across the lake. Then another. And another. When the count reached fifteen, Bean thought maybe a group of volunteers had arrived from Virginia City. But fires kept coming to life. When the number reached eighty, Bean was sure the Nez Perce had arrived.

The Madison scouts asked Bean what he was going to do. He replied that he expected a war party to come around the lake that night, so he was going to saddle up and go to the mountains to hide until morning. Bean and

This Nez Perce encampment along the Yellowstone River near the mouth of the Shields River was similar to the one attacked by the U.S. Army on the banks of the Big Hole River on August 9, 1877.

NATIONAL PARK SERVICE PHOTO BY WILLIAM HENRY JACKSON, 1871

Herendeen waited for the others to get their horses. Then everybody went two miles to a spot hidden in the timber. There Bean kept watch on the Nez Perce camp with his field glasses. From that spot he could see if the Indians would go down the Madison River toward the settlements or over Targhee Pass toward Yellowstone Park. Bean wanted to make sure which way they were headed.

Bean said, "We seen them pack up and start out toward the geyser country. When we were thoroughly satisfied which way they were going, our next move was to go to Virginia [City] and telegraph John Gibbon what we had seen."[9]

Bean was certain Indians had come around the lake by the next morning, so he and his companions had to keep hidden. When a bear approached their camp, they shooed it away with their hats, not daring to fire a shot.

It was about 9 o'clock by the time Bean and Herendeen started their rush for Virginia City. The town was sixty-five miles away, and they wanted to be there before the telegraph office closed at 7 p.m.

They traveled hidden in the timber for several miles and then turned onto the main road. As they hurried along, they encountered a group of eight miners from the Madison Valley mining town of Pony, who planned to steal horses from the Indians.[10] Nez Perce horses were among the best in the region, and apparently the miners figured they were fair game because the Indians were running away from their reservation.

Bean said, "We told them where the Indian camp was and they were disappointed that the camp had moved farther on."[11] Bean told the men to go back to a creek to spend the night. And he warned the men to "tie their horses up short" so they wouldn't be stolen.

"They had fine fat ponies and disregarded our advice and picketed them and put out one guard,"[12] Bean added.

"About 11 o'clock at night some Indians came over the hill—about four or five of them—and with their stampeding yells, they dashed through the camp," Bean said. "The guard fired once. Four of their horses broke loose and went with the Indians."[13]

Later a group of soldiers met the miners who were walking back to Pony. As one writer put it, the miners "had gone out to shear and come back shorn."[14]

Bean and Herendeen hurried to Virginia City and arrived there on August 23 just before the telegraph office was scheduled to close. They sent a telegram to Colonel Gibbon that read: *Indians were camped yesterday at Henrys Lake and moved up geyser road the same day. They had 1,500 head of stock. H. & B.*[15]

Then the exhausted scouts rode east out of Virginia City through a narrow valley where spring water supported aspen groves and lush grass. They picketed their hungry horses to graze and lay down to catch up on lost sleep. The next day while they rode over the pass and down the Madison Valley toward Bozeman, Bean and Herendeen met a squad of soldiers who demanded that they turn around and accompany them. Bean said he refused by telling the soldiers, "We had all the scouting we wanted for the present."[16] Bean and Herendeen then rode on to Bozeman.

CHAPTER 5

The Reluctant Guide

In the middle of the nineteenth century, a man armed with little more than a pick and shovel could make a fortune in the gold fields of the American West—and thousands of men tried. John Shively was one of them. In 1852, nineteen-year-old Shively left his home in Pennsylvania to seek his fortune in California.

Shively followed the gold rushes from California to Arizona and Nevada. About 1870 he arrived in Montana, where he spent six years building stamp mills that pounded ore into powder to extract minerals. In May 1877, he found himself in Deadwood, Dakota Territory. The gold rush there was ending, so he decided to join a group of thirty-one men headed to Wyoming to look for gold in one of the last areas in the country to be searched. After arduous months of digging drainage ditches and sinking test holes down to bedrock across central Wyoming, the prospectors had little to show for their efforts. They found only traces of gold in the Bighorn Mountains.

When they moved farther south to the Owl Creek Range, they found a quartz outcropping that looked encouraging and collected samples. The prospectors' provisions were running out, so they sent the samples to be assayed in Salt Lake City and disbanded. Shively waited for the assay results, but they turned out to be negative.

Undaunted, Shively joined five men who had heard from a Shoshone Indian who said he found a gold nugget worth $20 on a tributary south of Yellowstone Lake. The Shoshone guided the prospectors westward into the park for four days, but when they reached the Snake River area, he suddenly remembered he had pressing business back home. For a $10 fee, the Indian guided the prospectors another half day and pointed them to a mountain where the gold creek was supposed to be. Then he handed the prospectors a map and departed.

The prospectors found the creek the Indian had described, but after searching the stream and all its tributaries, they found nothing. Shively's companions decided to head back to civilization, but he continued on alone. He found some deposits that he thought might lead to gold and tried for three days to trace them. Finally, with his food running out, he decided to end his prospecting career. In disgust, he marched to the shore of Lake Yellowstone and hurled his pick and shovel into the waves.

Shively decided it was time to return to Montana and resume his career building and running stamp mills. Although he was running out of food, he decided to see Yellowstone's grand geysers, which were on the way.

With only two horses for companions, Shively headed around the south end of Lake Yellowstone, crossed the Yellowstone River, and headed over the Mary Mountain Trail. After he crossed Mary Mountain, he heard a group of men coming toward him. He stepped out from behind some bushes and hailed them.[1] The group included Frank Carpenter and two companions from the Radersburg Party, A. J. Arnold and William Dingee. They were traveling with a Yellowstone guide, George Huston, and his clients, who were on their way to the Yellowstone Lake and falls. When Shively asked the men if they had any food to spare, Huston told him no. But Arnold said there was plenty at the Radersburg Party's permanent camp at the Lower Geyser Basin, and he could help himself. With that news, Shively hurried away.

After restocking his food supply from the Radersburg cache, Shively headed up the Firehole River to see the geysers. At the Upper Geyser Basin, Shively found the camp of the Radersburg Party where Emma Cowan prepared a noon meal for him. While he was enjoying his first real conversation in weeks, his horses wandered away. When he discovered the horses were gone, he fired a shot to get the attention of the Radersburg Party and explain his plight. The Radersburg tourists agreed to take him and his equipment back to civilization.

With a belly full of lady-cooked food and a plan to get home, Shively left the Radersburg Party at the Upper Geyser Basin and ambled back to his camp at the Lower Basin. There was plenty to see as he made his way down the Firehole River. The water heated by geysers and springs wanders through lush, green meadows and past bare banks made white by geyser deposits.

Along the way Shively passed the Midway Geyser Basin, which had two of the largest geothermal features in the world. Grand Prismatic Spring was a steaming pool nearly 370 feet in diameter, whose stunning colors gave it its name. A rainbow was arranged in concentric circles from the outside inward:

red, orange, yellow, green, and blue. The other massive feature at Midway Basin was the world's largest geyser, the Excelsior.[2] Nobody knew when the Excelsior might erupt. But when it did it could thrust a three-hundred-foot column of water three hundred feet into the air and hurl stones the size of a man's head for a quarter of a mile.

The Excelsior just steamed and poured thousands of gallons of hot water down the bank of the Firehole River on the day Shively made his way back to his camp at the Lower Geyser Basin. When he got there, he leaned his rifle against a tree, kindled a fire, and prepared his dinner. He was just sitting down to eat when he heard a noise. Shively looked up and saw a young Indian named Yellow Wolf and his cousin spring up from the tall grass ten feet away. Shively leaped for his gun only to discover that twenty or thirty men surrounded him.

Shively asked the men their tribe. "Sioux," they replied.

"You are not Sioux,"[3] Shively said. He was fresh from Sioux country in the Black Hills, so he knew that Sioux plucked their eyebrows. He saw that these men didn't.

"Nez Perce," the Indians then admitted.

The Indians began to talk loudly, gesticulate wildly, and flourish their pistols. Shively decided an exhibit of bravery might help his situation. He folded his arms across his chest and announced that he was not afraid to die.

An Indian placed his hand on Shively's chest and held it there. After a minute, the man announced, "hyas skukum tum tum."[4] Shively understood enough of the Indians' language to know that meant "strong heart." While this was happening, the Indians confiscated all of Shively's belongings and ordered him to mount an old, white horse. Then they led him down to the main body of Nez Perce that was coming up the river.

As darkness fell a full moon came out, and the Indians took Shively to a spot where a council of chiefs was meeting. They thrust him into the center of the council circle, where the chiefs asked who he was and where he came from. More important, they asked if he knew the area well enough to guide them through the park, and if he was willing to do that. Shively's prospecting gave him a good knowledge of the park and he figured being a guide was preferable to being shot, so he agreed to show the Nez Perce the way to Crow Country.

The chiefs asked if there was good grass ahead, and Shively told them there was. They put him back on the old, white horse and moved to the prairie near the place where his campfire had revealed him to his captors. There the Nez Perce made their own camp.

At the new camp, the Indians treated Shively as a guest and gave him a blanket and a meal of camas root and willow tea. They placed Shively under the custody of a man called Joe Hale, also known as Poker Joe or Lean Elk.[5] Shively thought someone had ordered Poker Joe to watch him, but actually Poker Joe was in charge of travel plans and daily activities of all the Nez Perce at that time, although the chiefs' council always convened for a big decision. He was the chief of a small Nez Perce band, and the chiefs' council had chosen him to lead the tribe through Yellowstone Park because he knew the area.

Poker Joe, who had lived with his band near Missoula for years, spoke English well. Shively and Poker Joe chatted through the evening. Poker Joe said he wanted to be Shively's friend and advised the prospector not to run away. Poker Joe said the Indians decided to travel through Yellowstone Park to avoid the army. Their normal route to the buffalo country on the eastern Montana plains would have taken them down the Madison River and east toward Bozeman, directly toward the army garrison at Fort Ellis.

Poker Joe told Shively the Nez Perce knew they could get to Crow country through the park, but they weren't familiar with the exact route. If Shively would keep his promise to guide them, Poker Joe said, he would be treated well and eventually set free. Shively knew he had no choice, so he promised to do everything the Indians asked.

The next morning, August 24, the Indians put Shively on a good horse and took him to the head of their caravan. He led them up Nez Perce Creek, a stream that led to Mary Mountain. At the foot of the mountain, the entourage stopped for a noon meal. There the Radersburg Party, which the Indians had captured at the Lower Geyser Basin that morning, was brought in and forced to trade their fine horses for the Indians' worn-out animals.

While the horse trading was going on, Poker Joe sent Shively ahead to lead an advance party over the mountain. When Shively got a mile from the camp, he heard several gunshots ring out behind him and assumed the Indians were executing the Radersburg Party.

That night at camp near the Mud Volcano, Shively heard the Indians arguing about prisoners. The next morning he saw thirteen-year-old Ida Carpenter coming toward him. Soon Poker Joe brought Ida's sister, Emma Cowan, to Ida. Ida threw herself into Emma's arms with tears of joy at finding her sister still alive.[6] Shively told the sisters about his conversations with Poker Joe and tried to reassure them that they would be released. But Emma was still distressed.

A newspaper that later reported Shively's story paraphrased him: "Through this terrible ordeal, the sisters behaved nobly and with utmost fortitude although Mrs. Cowan's mental agony at the thought of her husband wounded and perhaps dead, and they three at the hands of savages was enough to have driven her distracted."[7]

Poker Joe left the group and began circling the camp, giving orders for the day's march. Frank Carpenter then arrived leading four horses, one for each of the siblings and one for Shively. The four rode together past Mud Geyser.

Frank looked toward the Yellowstone River and saw a white man surrounded by Indians and went to talk with him.[8] The captured man was James Irwin, who was hiding in a washout when the Indians captured him. He had recently been discharged from the army at Fort Ellis. Shively said Irwin was wearing army blue trousers, so he thought the man was a deserter, a conclusion he shared with Emma Cowan.[9]

Irwin started to tell Frank that the Helena Party was hidden in a camp about six miles away. Frank winked at Irwin and got him to stop talking, but not before the Indians learned about the other tourists.[10] The Indians would raid the Helena tourists' camp the next day, stealing their horses and leaving one of them dead.

The Indians moved to the banks of the Yellowstone River where Frank watched them plunge in and make their way across. Soon Frank and his sisters also crossed. Their horses had to swim the deep water, and the siblings got wet.

Later that day, a council of chiefs convened to decide what to do with the captives. After the chiefs deliberated for a while, Poker Joe announced the Indians would free them. The Indians put the sisters on worn-out horses but decided their brother, Frank Carpenter, would have to walk. Then Poker Joe took them back across the Yellowstone River and set them free.

After the siblings departed, Shively told Poker Joe that he had $35 and wanted to buy a horse. Joe brought him an old pony with a good saddle and bridle, and a deal was made. Then the entourage moved about four miles and camped at the north end of Lake Yellowstone.

About 9 p.m., four young men on horseback galloped into camp, firing their rifles to announce their return from a raid on the Helena Party. The Indians had overheard the captured ex-soldier, James Irwin, tell Frank Carpenter about the Helena tourists. The returning raiders had killed one man and drove his companions into the wilderness. Most of the refugees headed back toward McCartney's cabin at Mammoth Hot Springs, but two fled southward toward the geysers along the Firehole River.

As soon as the Indians heard the shots of the returning raiders, everybody—old men, women, and children—grabbed guns and rushed toward the shooting. Although it turned out to be a false alarm, Shively could see that all the Indians were willing and able to fight. The commotion soon turned into a celebration of the raiders' safe return and their capture of fourteen fine horses.

Shively showed the Indians a route over the rugged mountains to Crow country, but the chief of a group of Snake Indians traveling with the Nez Perce said he knew an easier way. The chiefs' council relieved Shively of guide duty and put him to work along with Irwin clearing the trail. Shively could see that the Nez Perce were traveling in a circle, but he said nothing. When the Indians finally figured out they were lost, they called another council and reinstated Shively, who again pointed them to a rugged route over the mountains with no trail.

The Indians followed Shively's advice and made their way to the top of a divide following up a mountain stream. The next morning, Irwin pointed to another stream that flowed downward and asked Shively where it went. Shively told him it led to the Lamar River that ran toward Mammoth Hot Springs. Irwin then got permission to go for a drink and made his getaway. That evening when the Indians noticed Irwin was gone, Poker Joe told Shively he didn't care. But he advised Shively, "If you try, I get heap mad."[11]

It rained the following afternoon, and Poker Joe invited Shively to spend the night in his lodge. But Shively said he preferred to sleep under the trees and would make himself a shelter there. He made a show of fixing himself a place and turned in. He waited for an hour, and then got up. Looking around, he took his bearings from the North Star. Then he slipped away.

First he headed south directly away from the Indians' camp, and he then circled north around the horses, before heading east. Shively was proud of his stealth, but the Indians later said they let him slip away because they were almost through the park and in familiar country, so they didn't need him anymore. The Indians said they intended to release Shively the next day after returning his property and paying him handsomely for his services.[12]

By daybreak, Shively had crossed a small divide and could see the Soda Butte, an extinct geyser cone near the east end of the Lamar Valley. He walked fifteen miles to Soda Butte and followed the Lamar River another fifteen miles to its confluence with the Yellowstone. There he crossed the charred ruins of Baronett's Bridge, which Nez Perce scouts had set on fire to slow the progress of General O. O. Howard's pursuing army. At the bridge he found the carcass of a hawk that Howard's couriers had left by a campfire. He cooked the hawk and ate it as he trudged on. He pronounced it delicious.

When he arrived at McCartney's cabin at Mammoth Hot Springs, he found a burning fire in the stove and a few potatoes that had been left in a pot, probably by soldiers who came to McCartney's cabin to bury the body of Richard Dietrich, a member of the Helena Party who Nez Perce raiders had killed five days before. Soldiers had placed Dietrich's body in a tin tub to make a temporary burial. Shively didn't know the grave was just a few yards away when he wrapped himself in an abandoned quilt and slept.

The next morning, he walked farther north to Henderson's Ranch, where Nez Perce scouts had attacked five days before. The scouts fled when Lieutenant Gustavus Doane arrived with troops and a contingent of Crow Indians he had recruited to fight the Nez Perce.

Shively saw that the ranch house had been burned, but chickens were running around a stable that was still standing. He found a nest of eggs, made a fire, and cooked them. He then discovered a cache of flour, bacon, and sugar and started to make bread. A man returning from the Clarks Fork Mines arrived and helped Shively get back to civilization. When he arrived at Fort Ellis, he told his story to army officials there.

Shively then went from Bozeman to Helena and to Deer Lodge, where he told his story to *The New Northwest* newspaper. After that he went to Butte to look for a job as a millwright.

CHAPTER 6

Frolic in Geyserland

When the Radersburg Party finally reached the Lower Geyser Basin, they were overcome with an urge to see the sights. Emma Cowan said her husband, George, always insisted on making camp before doing anything else: "Putting up tents, gathering fragrant pine boughs for camp beds, getting things in regular housekeeping order. But the sight of geysers and the smell of sulfurous steam from nearby springs made us simply wild with the eagerness of seeing all things at once,"[1] so George relaxed his make-camp-first rule.

The travelers left their teams in harness and ran to see the sights. They dashed from place to place, calling each other to come and see every new wonder. Emma and Ida couldn't keep up with the men, but they didn't care. They found plenty to interest them, such as the paint pots—depressions in the earth where hot gas bubbled through thick mud that popped and splattered like boiling pudding.

Emma tossed a stick into a paint pot and watched the bubbling goo suck it out of sight. She thought of the possibility of someone falling in and shuddered. When the women stopped to rest, Emma recounted to Ida about the wondrous tales Gilman Sawtell, the man who built the compound where they stayed at Henrys Lake, told her when she was a little girl—tales of deep springs that shimmered in all the colors of the rainbow and of geysers that spouted boiling water skyward.

The women were content taking in wonders nearby, but Frank had to see everything. He climbed a knoll and looked northward a mile. "From this point," he said, "I had an excellent view of the whole basin. Its many geysers, constantly spouting forth their columns of steam, gave it the appearance of a large manufacturing town."[2] He left the knoll and crossed a ridge to a point where he could view the entire Lower Geyser Basin. There he saw dozens of hot springs and geysers that spouted up to thirty feet.

Frank thought everything needed to be poked and probed and measured. Such information would be useful for the book he was planning to write. He used a tree from the nearby lodgepole forest to probe the paint pots and determined they were between four and thirty feet deep. When he found a large crater filled with hot, bubbling mud that he dubbed "the Devil's Mud Pot," he shoved his thirty-foot pole into its repulsive mouth. The mud pot slowly sucked the pole out of sight. Then with a loud thump, it hurled the pole out and sent a spout of mud fifteen feet into the air. Gobs of mud flew everywhere and splashed to the ground.

The sun was beginning to set when the travelers reined in their curiosity and discovered they were far from where their horses waited. They retraced their steps to the horses and found a spot to set up tents. The camp they set up that night wasn't up to their usual standards, but nobody complained.

Emma said, "We were hungry and tired, but altogether happy. We had realized our expectations."[3]

The next morning, Dingee's dolorous yell "grub pile" roused the travelers to their first morning in geyserland. The sun shone brightly, and the cool morning air was still. The first order of business was to set up a permanent camp closer to the geysers. The group moved about two miles and camped in a grove of pines.

After setting up camp, they walked about half a mile to the Fountain Geyser. When the travelers arrived, the surface of the geyser pool was still, and rainbow tints reflected from its surface. As the sun rose, the tints changed and reflections of the white clouds that floated in the sky appeared.

As the tourists watched, a white bubble emerged from a dark hole in the deepest part of the pool, rose to the surface, and exploded. Another bubble followed, and another. The bubbles came faster and faster and the pool's surface began to boil. Finally, a waterspout erupted with a rushing noise.

Frank said the geyser "spouts forty or fifty feet in the air, throwing its columns in different directions in each spout. It is now boiling at a fearful rate and the mind of one involuntarily reverts to the story of Satan and his imps, pounding, thumping and pumping brimstone with infernal ingenuity."[4]

The ground under the watchers' feet trembled for nearly an hour; then it stood still. The water subsided and the pool calmed. Soon the surface eased back to stillness and reflected the white clouds passing overhead. After the

Fountain Geyser subsided, the group dispersed and people wandered from sight to sight.

The geyser basin had no signs to direct sightseers, no boardwalks to carry them safely over the thin crust that covered the boiling water below, and no rangers to keep them from defacing the delicate geothermal features. The travelers went where they wished to the very edges of tranquil and beautiful pools that sometimes turned to seething caldrons and hurled boiling water high into the air. They harvested specimens: the delicate geothermal lace that edged pools, geyser eggs that rolled about in the turbulent water, and colorful crystals that formed where boiling water cooled.

When Philetus W. Norris became superintendent of Yellowstone Park in 1877, he immediately issued regulations that forbid collecting specimens, defacing natural features, and wantonly destroying wildlife. But the federal government didn't give Norris any resources to hire rangers to enforce his regulations, so most people ignored them—including well-heeled tourists like the members of the Radersburg Party.

George Cowan, who was the county attorney for Jefferson County, Montana, strode around the geyser basins collecting specimens and adding his name beside those he found carved on geothermal features. George found hundreds of well-preserved names written with lead pencils on the sides of formations, some of them dated as far back as 1866.[5]

Inspecting graffiti wasn't safe. Once when George stepped into a geyser crater to add his name to others there, boiling waters suddenly began to rise and he had to scramble to safety.

Not everyone avoided being scalded. The driver of the supply wagon, Henry Meyers, let the wonders of the area divert his attention from where he was walking and stepped into a hot spring. Frank heard Meyers's agonized cry and rushed across the chalky crust to help him. Meyers yelled out a stream of expletives and hopped toward Frank on one foot, holding the other in his hands.

After Frank arrived, Meyers pulled up his pant leg and began rolling down his sock. Skin and flesh stuck to the material, exposing the young man's raw nerves, and he writhed in agony.

When Meyers calmed down, Frank asked, "Was the spring hot?"

"Yes, damn you," Meyers replied.[6]

Frank rushed away and sent a horse to haul Meyers back to camp where his injuries were bandaged. After Meyers was made as comfortable as possible, the travelers had supper, told each other what they had seen that day, and went to bed.

After breakfast on August 17, the Radersburg Party decided to cache most of their supplies and leave their wagons at what they called their permanent camp. In 1873, Virginia City merchants had hired Gilman Sawtell to build the road from his compound to the park to capitalize on the tourist trade. Sawtell's road ended at the Lower Geyser Basin, so the travelers had to go to the Upper Geyser Basin on horseback.

While the party was getting ready to leave, they were surprised to see three men and a boy ride into camp. It was a group of tourists led by George Huston, a Yellowstone pioneer who had been exploring the area for nearly fifteen years.

In 1864, Huston led two parties of forty prospectors into the area that became Yellowstone National Park. The first expedition went up the Yellowstone River, and the second up the Madison. The prospecting groups had to be large because they needed enough men to repel Indian attacks. The fear of Indians was well founded. Just a year before, a group of prospectors left Bannack to search for gold in the lower Yellowstone Valley. Crow Indians attacked and forced them to return over the Oregon Trail, a sixteen-hundred-mile detour. A second group that had planned to travel with the first also encountered Crow Indians, who took their horses and turned them back. On their return trip to Bannack, the second group discovered gold in Alder Gulch, triggering the giant rush that established Virginia City, one of the richest gold strikes in history.

Frank Carpenter said when Huston met the Radersburg Party, he gave "the particulars of the Big Hole Fight. The first we had heard about it."[7] It's not clear how Huston knew about the bloody fight between the Nez Perce and the army, but his information was out of date. He didn't know the Nez Perce were approaching the park as he spoke. He even said he didn't think the tourists were in any danger because the Indians feared geysers—an assertion that proved false just a few days later. Emma Cowan erroneously attributed news of the battle to scouts from "the Sherman party."[8]

The Radersburg Party was delighted to have an experienced guide like Huston, so the two groups merged. When the travelers got to the Upper Basin and began pitching their tents, Huston yelled, "There she goes!" Half a mile away Old Faithful made a rumbling noise and thrust a column of water 150 feet into the air. The campers dropped everything and began to run toward the eruption, but Huston advised them another one would come in just sixty-five minutes, so they decided to wait and finished setting up their camp.[9]

The tourists minded their watches, and when the predicted time approached they headed toward Old Faithful. They found the geyser in the center of a white mound about thirty feet high surrounded by tiny ponds that caught water when the geyser played. As the tourists drew near, the ground began to rumble; then water rose six feet and subsided; then it rose and subsided again. With each cycle the geyser gained strength until with a rushing sound it hurled water upward 150 feet. After playing fifteen minutes, Old Faithful collapsed and rested. The tourists continued their tour and got to see other geysers playing—including the Giantess and the Beehive.

Emma and George had pitched their tent in a point of timber close to Castle Geyser. Emma said that night after they went to bed the geyser "gave a mighty eruption, covering us with spray and making the most unearthly noise. I was sure the earth would be rent asunder and we would be swallowed up."[10]

Frank, who had stayed up to watch geysers play in the moonlight, had a different opinion. "Standing in the shadow of the jet of steam," he said, "we have one of the most strikingly beautiful views that ever the eye of man beheld. It seems like a solid column of silver. The steam soon passes away and soon again stillness reigns."[11]

The next morning Emma and George walked around the Castle's white cone. By then the geyser was calm, and all they could see was a huge column of steam. During their stay, Castle erupted five times, but Emma said it wasn't nearly as terrifying in daylight as it had been that first night.

The next morning the travelers experimented making geyser coffee, cooking potatoes, and washing dishes in a hot spring. Then they spread out to see the sights, gathered specimens of rocks, crystals and vegetation, and carved their names on thermal features.

August 19 was a Sunday, and the party resolved to take a day of rest. But lolling around camp grew boring, so they decided to do laundry. After all, there were thousands of gallons of hot water around.

Huston apparently had mastered the secrets of doing laundry in a geyser during his years as a prospector and guide. Loose garments tossed in a resting geyser he knew would be shredded on sharp, rocky surfaces underground. But if they were bundled and hurled in as the geyser began to spout, the maelstrom would swirl them in boiling water, carry them skyward, and drop them on the chalky ground below.

Emma and Ida filled a pillowcase with their dainties. Dingee tied a rock to his shirt. And Arnold took off his dirty jacket. Then they all adjourned to the laundry—Old Faithful.

They waited at the edge of the geyser and listened for the gurgling of the water. When the geyser made its first thrust, pushing water a few feet above the surface, Huston yelled at the tourists to throw their bundles into the vortex. The water receded, and the tourists waited. As time passed, they began to think they would never see their clothing again.

In the next instant, Old Faithful spouted with a roar and hurled the bundles a hundred feet in the air and splashed them into the basins below. When the boiling water receded, the tourists fished out their clothing and, in Frank's phrase, found it "as nice and clean as a Chinaman could wash it."[12]

The success with laundry prompted Frank and his friends to experiment more. They gathered rubble like boulders and tree stumps and dumped them into the geyser cone. They kept shoving rubble into the cone until the geyser was due to play again. Then they sat down to watch the show.

Sixty-five minutes after the previous eruption, the ground began to tremble. Then, as Frank described it, "Off she goes and away go rocks, trees, and rubbish to a height of seventy-five or eighty in the air."[13]

Frank added, "Old Faithful seems to have been angered by such an unwarrantable procedure on our parts, or wishes to show us how futile are our attempts to check his power, and furnishes entertainment of unusual magnitude and duration."[14]

That evening when Huston announced that he was taking his party north, Frank, Arnold, and Dingee jumped at the opportunity to go with an experienced guide to the lake, Grand Canyon, and falls of the Yellowstone. The rest of the party decided to stay at the Upper Geyser Basin and meet Frank and his friends at the Lower Basin on August 22.

Castle Geyser erupted just as the men left for the Lower Geyser Basin to pick up supplies at the permanent camp where the trail over Mary Mountain began. On their trip the men would not only see marvelous sights, they would meet a curious mix of tourists: a wealthy Bozeman businessman who made his fortune driving Texas longhorns to Montana, a flamboyant show-man and sometime partner of Buffalo Bill Cody who was guiding two Eng-lishmen, and a prospector from the Black Hills who had been searching the park for gold.

When Frank and his companions arrived at the permanent camp, they heard a growling beast. It turned out to be George Cowan's dog, Dido, who had been guarding the baggage since the party left for the Upper Basin. She had ridden the wagon all the way from Radersburg and regarded it as her home. At first, Dido tried to keep the group from approaching the wagon, but when she saw that Frank was riding George's horse, she acquiesced.

Dingee stocked provisions for four days and the group headed out. They went up what Frank called the East Fork of the Firehole. Now it's known as Nez Perce Creek because it is the route the Indians took a few days later when they crossed from the drainage of the Madison River to the Yellow-stone River.

The group had gone ten miles up Nez Perce Creek when a man startled them by stepping out of the bushes onto the trail. Frank described him as a "wretched looking specimen of humanity,"[15] and Huston grabbed for his gun. But the stranger offered a friendly greeting and introduced himself as John Shively. Shively, who had been prospecting for gold in the park, asked for provisions. Huston said the group had none to share, but A. J. Arnold told the prospector the Radersburg permanent camp was a few miles away at the Lower Geyser Basin and said he could help himself there. With that information, Shively rushed away.

The group traveled thirty miles over the mountain to a creek fed by hot springs and camped. The next morning Arnold went fishing since he knew they had crossed into the Yellowstone drainage away from the fishless Fire-hole River. He caught a half dozen little fish with small, red spots on their sides. Huston said the fish were found nowhere else because the species was trapped between the mountains and hot springs below.

After eating the fish for breakfast, the group rode toward Yellowstone Lake. After about four miles, they encountered another group of tourists that was led by Nelson Story, a Bozeman businessman who made his fortune driving a thousand longhorn steers from Texas to Montana to sell beef to ravenous miners near Virginia City and later became one of the richest men in Montana, owning thousands of cattle, flour mills, steamboats, and other businesses. Story and his group went on their way to see the geysers.

Frank and his companions passed Mud Geyser about a half mile west of the Yellowstone River.[16] Frank said that when this fifty-foot pool erupted, it sent gobs of mud that could sear the skin like hot sealing wax.[17] As they went along, Huston pointed out thermal features, giving them colorful names like "Arsenic Springs" and "The Devil's Well."

While they trotted along at a brisk canter, they saw a man driving a herd of loose horses. The man rode by without stopping. Then they saw another man, one Frank described as "tall and powerfully built." This man rode along carelessly carrying his rifle across his saddle. He was dressed head to toe in buckskin and wore a wide, brimmed sombrero with an eagle feather, a red neckerchief, and beaded moccasins.

This was John Baker Omohundro, better known as "Texas Jack." Texas Jack was born on a Virginia plantation but went to Texas in his early teens to become a cowboy and earned his nickname there. When the Civil War broke out, Texas Jack returned to Virginia to fight for the Confederacy. He was too young to be a soldier, but when officers discovered he was familiar with the contested areas of Virginia they made him a courier and scout.

After the Civil War, he returned to the West, where he met Buffalo Bill Cody and worked with him as a buffalo hunter supplying meat for railroad crews building the first transcontinental railroad and as a guide for wealthy tourists from Europe and the East. In 1872, Texas Jack and Buffalo Bill starred in a Ned Buntline Wild West show, "The Scouts of the Prairie." They interspersed their show business activities with guiding hunting expeditions for American military men and European gentry. Texas Jack met the Earl of Dunraven when he guided the wealthy Irishman on a hunting expedition on the plains. When Dunraven decided to see the wonders of Yellowstone Park in 1874, he hired Texas Jack to guide him. Dunraven immortalized their Yellowstone trip in his book *The Great Divide*, which helped popularize the park in Europe.

Huston knew Texas Jack and talked with him while the others stared at the famous celebrity. When Jack asked if Huston had any "spare grub," Huston said he didn't, but Nelson Story and his party were just ahead and he should ask them. Jack bid adieu and left.

Huston led his party to a summit and stopped. He told the party he had been to this spot for ten years in a row, and he always tarried at the place to admire the view of Lake Yellowstone. The group stopped for several minutes to admire the scene that Frank said was "a thousand feet below us, stretching away to the south 30 miles, [and where] lie[s] the placid waters of Yellowstone Lake. It is so calm that it looks like a huge mirror surrounded by verdure covered mountains that tower thousands of feet above it."[18]

The party found a nice place to camp in a pine grove near a cold spring about two hundred feet above the lake. The hungry men built a fire and fixed a meal out of their supplies. Frank said the familiar call—"grub pile"—was never sweeter.

Dingee sat in the grass, took a bite of the bread they had made, and immediately spit it out. Frank said he then threw out "one prolonged sulfurous oath."[19] While Dingee kept swearing, the other men gingerly sampled the bread, which turned out to be mostly salt.

Dingee indignantly asked Frank if he had added salt to the flour when the men stocked supplies at the base camp, and Frank confessed that he had added one cup. Then Frank added that he had put in four cups of sugar to sweeten the mix. Then it dawned on Frank that the second addition came from the salt sack. Arnold then recalled that he too had added two cups of "sugar." In all, the men figured, they had added six pints of salt to eighteen pounds of flour—and condemned themselves to a choice between short rations or salty bread.

After supper, Arnold went fishing to augment their meager food stock. Everyone else walked along the lakeshore collecting petrified wood and rock specimens. In the book Frank published a year later, he joked that if he had known that everything he collected would wind up in "Chief Joseph's cabinet," he wouldn't have been so diligent in his collecting.

The men came to a deserted log house and found a derelict sailboat, but they decided they weren't staying long enough to bother fixing it. Later they discovered a rowboat in a nearby slough and dragged it to the lake to go fishing. Using grasshoppers for bait, they caught several eighteen-to-twenty-inch trout.

After they returned to shore, Huston noticed a storm rising and told the group they were in for a spectacular scene. Soon waves began to roll across the lake and turn into whitecaps as they approached the shore. Gulls and pelicans rode the crests and sailed away with shrill cries that mingled with the sounds of the crashing waves and wind. Frank said the sound was blood curdling and was grateful that the group was not on the lake in the sailboat. Soon, Dingee's call of "grub pile" rose above the roar and summoned everyone to eat.

After supper the group discovered that in their eagerness to watch the lake storm, they had neglected to picket their horses—and the animals were gone. They immediately began a search and kept looking until 10 o'clock when they gave up convinced that someone had stolen the horses. Only a lonely pack mule remained, and he spent the night braying and tugging on his picket rope trying to follow his companions.

At daybreak, the group resumed their search for the missing horses. Frank remained in camp to prepare breakfast. When he had the food ready, he yelled "grub pile." Then the men returned to camp—without the horses. They were glum at the prospect of having to walk more than thirty-five miles over mountainous terrain with only a braying mule to carry their dwindling supplies and salty flour.

After breakfast, the men spread out in all directions to look for the missing horses with no luck. Then the mule's incessant racket gave Frank an idea. He figured the lonely creature might be able to find the missing horses and suggested turning him loose. Huston immediately climbed on the mule's back and gave it free rein. Half an hour later, Huston returned with the missing horses. After cheers of celebration, the men packed up to go to Yellowstone Falls.

To get to the falls, they needed to retrace their route to the spot where they first saw the lake. When they got there, they turned to take one last look. The storm of the night before had passed and the lake was placid and smooth, reflecting the morning sun like a mirror.

They traveled quickly past Sulphur Mountain and Alum Creek. It was nearly three o'clock before they stopped to eat. Although they were hungry, they carefully picketed their horses before dining. After dinner, they walked five hundred feet to view the canyon and Lower Falls. They found a good viewing spot and sat down to watch the water pound down three hundred feet to the bottom of the thousand-foot-deep canyon.

After an hour, they returned to camp where Huston announced that he and his clients were continuing to Mammoth Hot Springs. Then the guide and his clients headed north leaving Frank, Dingee, and Arnold to manage the return trip to the Lower Geyser Basin for themselves.

The trio went to see the Upper Falls and spent a cold night. On the morning of August 23, the men packed for their return trip. They chose a different route than they had taken to the falls so they could get back to the Lower Geyser Basin that afternoon. They were already a day late for the rendezvous they had promised their companions.

While Frank and his friends were returning, the rest of the party waited for them at their permanent camp in the Lower Geyser Basin. They were having a busy day meeting other tourists, Emma said the first she had seen in the park. John Shively, the prospector who Frank had met on his trip to the falls, joined them for breakfast. That afternoon, Shively came back to say his horses had wandered away while he was eating.

Then another party arrived at the Radersburg camp. In a reminiscence Emma Cowan wrote decades later, she said it was "General Sherman and party."[20] But that can't be right because the famous Civil War general was back to Fort Ellis just one day after the meeting Emma described and he couldn't possibly have traveled there that fast. Emma must have confused the general's party with one of the other groups that was visiting the park then. It could have been Texas Jack's group, but Emma probably would have noticed Jack's flamboyant sombrero and buckskins. Most likely it was the party of the wealthy Bozeman businessman, Nelson Story. Emma said the visitors she saw that day had entered via Mammoth Hot Springs like the Story Party. After Story returned to Bozeman, he told the newspaper that he had been at the Lower Geyser Basin the day before the Nez Perce arrived there.[21] Also, a prospector named William Harmon left the Story Party to return to the settlements with the Radersburg Party.

Whoever it was, Emma said, he told about the Big Hole Battle and left the impression that the travelers might encounter Indians on their way home. "We felt somewhat depressed and worried over the news,"[22] she said. The visitor also told the group that they would be safe in the geyser basin because Indians were afraid to come near there. But Emma said that didn't reassure her. "I observed," she said, "that his party preferred being elsewhere as they left the basin that same night."[23]

* * * *

54

Before Frank and his friends approached the Lower Geyser Basin, they decided to pretend to be Indians one more time to scare Emma and Ida. They decorated their horses with eagle feathers and galloped into camp with war whoops. The women weren't impressed and simply greeted them with the Indian salute, "How."

Dingee immediately asked for a meal with unsalted bread. Emma scurried around to accommodate him while the men recounted their adventures.

The party held a council and decided to start for home the next day. Emma said the women were worried about the Nez Perce, so the men built a huge bonfire, brought out the fiddle and guitar, and tried to cheer them up. The men "dressed up as brigands," Emma said, "with pistols, knives and guns strapped on them."[24]

"Al Oldham, with his swart complexion, wearing a broad sombrero, looked a typical one, showing off to good advantage before the glaring campfire."[25] Mann apparently agreed and got out his pencils and sketched the scene. The evening's entertainment climaxed with dancing, Dingee doing a "Pigeon Wing, and Arnold a 'Double Shuffle.'" Emma said, "They made the woods ring with their nonsense and merriment for some time."[26]

Emma, Ida, and George retired to their tent, but the men decided to sleep out under the trees. Frank noticed that Emma had been uneasy the whole evening, so he asked her what was wrong. "Nothing," she replied, but as Frank lay in his bedroll, he could see her come to the door of her tent over and over and look into the woods. Perhaps she was just checking to make sure the bonfire her friends had built to celebrate their impending departure from Yellowstone hadn't spread. Perhaps she was hoping to see Fountain Geyser play one more time. The bright moonlight reflected on the surrounding chalky ground would have made that a beautiful sight. But most likely, she was worried about encountering the Nez Perce on the trip home. She couldn't have known that a Nez Perce scout named Yellow Wolf and his friends had seen the bonfire and were planning to attack the camp the next morning.

While the Radersburg Party staged its minstrel show, a group of Nez Perce scouts was preparing their camp across the swampy flats across from their camp. The Indians' leader, a relative of Chief Joseph named Yellow Wolf, was out picketing his horse for the night when he saw the Radersburg bonfire flickering through the trees. He summoned his companions and pointed out the fire.

"It may be soldiers or other white people," Yellow Wolf said. "We will go see why it is."

But one of his companions replied, "We better not go there. It is a swampy place. Our horses might mire down, for we cannot see good."[27]

Yellow Wolf replied, "We will be right here till morning. Then we're going to have a fight with them."

CHAPTER 7
Radersburg Capture

Poker Joe was an unlikely candidate to lead the combined Nez Perce bands. But when the Nez Perce chiefs met to choose one of their peers to lead them, they sought the best man for the job at hand. After the Big Hole Battle, that job was guiding the tribe past army posts and settlements in western Montana to the buffalo country of the eastern plains. Poker Joe and his band had lived in the Bitterroot Valley of Montana for several years before he joined the fleeing Nez Perce, so he knew the routes through the Rocky Mountains. It didn't matter that Poker Joe's father was a French Canadian, or that he was chief of a band of only six lodges. The chiefs thought he was the best man for the job of choosing routes and supervising the travel of the combined Nez Perce. Of course, the council of chiefs made the major decisions.

The chiefs wanted to avoid conflict with whites, but they knew that many of their followers were eager for revenge after the army's sneak attack at the Big Hole where army officers ordered their men—both soldiers and civilian volunteers—to aim their rifles low at the sleeping Indians' tepees. The attackers' bullets killed dozens of women and children, and men who had lost wives and children were enraged enough to kill any white person they saw.

After the Big Hole Battle, Poker Joe led the Nez Perce away from their usual route to the buffalo country, which would have taken them near the towns of Bannack, Virginia City, and Bozeman, and more important, toward the army post at Fort Ellis. Instead he took them through an unsettled section of eastern Idaho and circled back to Montana. But groups of young men left the main troop and marauded in the Horse Prairie section of southwest Montana. When ranchers there heard Indians were coming, they sent their wives and children to the gold rush town of Bannack, where citizens barricaded themselves in the courthouse. They covered the courthouse windows with mattresses, hauled in barrels of water, and fortified a nearby well, but the Indians bypassed the town.[1]

Several men stayed at their ranches to put up hay and protect their property. That didn't work. The Indians attacked, ransacking houses for money and food and tearing apart feather mattresses, apparently to collect ticking to make bandages for the companions wounded at the Big Hole Battle. They killed five men and stole about forty horses. The horse thefts not only replenished the Nez Perce herds but also deprived the pursuing army of fresh mounts.

On August 23, 1877, Poker Joe led the Nez Perce from Henrys Lake over Targhee Pass up the Madison River and into Yellowstone Park. At the confluence of the Gibbon and Firehole rivers, they turned up the Firehole River. As the Indians approached the point where Nez Perce Creek[2] flowed into the Firehole, a group of young men brought a prospector they had captured to Poker Joe. The group led by a relative of Chief Joseph's named Yellow Wolf had entered the park a day ahead of the main body of Nez Perce. Patrols like Yellow Wolf's were common after the Big Hole Battle. They ranged around the main body of Indians as much as thirty miles, taking revenge on whites and looking for horses to steal. When the Nez Perce passed through Yellowstone Park, such patrols wreaked havoc by attacking tourists and stealing horses. One group attacked a ranch north of Mammoth Hot Springs and exchanged gunshots with its owners. They set buildings on fire and made off with horses. On their way to rejoin the main Nez Perce group, they burned Baronett's Bridge, the only bridge across the Yellowstone River at the time.

* * * *

As Yellow Wolf and his companions approached the Lower Geyser Basin, they heard someone chopping wood. They sneaked up and grabbed the woodchopper. Soon other Indians arrived and one of them, a half-blood called Charley, who could speak English, interrogated the man. He was John Shively, who had been prospecting for gold all over Yellowstone Park. Charley discovered Shively could be forced to serve as a guide to help the Indians find their way across the park. Yellow Wolf and his companions decided to take the prospector to the chiefs and let them decide what to do with him.

After sending Shively away, Yellow Wolf continued his scouting trip with four men. That evening while they were setting up camp, a firelight flickering through the trees in the distance caught their attention. They looked closely and saw the bonfire that the Radersburg Party had started to celebrate their plan to leave the park the next day. Yellow Wolf and his companions knew the area was too swampy to cross in the dark, so they decided to wait until morning to investigate. They picketed their horses and bedded down for the night. They didn't even make a campfire so they wouldn't be spotted.

At dawn the next morning, Yellow Wolf woke his companions. The young men mounted their horses and rode through a draw to the grove where they had seen the bonfire through the trees the night before. When they arrived, they stayed hidden in the trees to assess the situation. They saw four men rolled up in blankets under a tree about eight feet from a campfire ring, and two more lying under another tree. A small tent nearby sheltered George Cowan, his wife, Emma, and her sister, Ida Carpenter. In the background, steam rose into the cool morning air from the hot springs and geysers of the Lower Basin.

The scouts stayed hidden in the trees and quietly discussed what to do next. Yellow Wolf said, "These people were not soldiers, but all white people seemed our enemies. We talked what to do with them. I said we would kill them."[3]

But one of his companions argued: "No, we will capture them. Take them to the chiefs. Whatever they say will go."[4]

While the Indians debated, William Dingee and A. J. Arnold got up to light the campfire and started cooking breakfast. Dingee took a coffee pot and a pail to fetch water from a nearby stream. After he had walked a few yards, he glanced up and saw three Indians sitting on horses. After the Indians were discovered, they got off their horses and walked into the camp and greeted Dingee: "How."[5]

"How," Dingee replied. Then he asked what tribe the Indians belonged to.

"Snakes," one replied, but Dingee said, "No," and told the Indians he knew that was wrong. When they admitted they were Nez Perce, Dingee asked if their chief was Joseph.

They laughed and said, "Yes, do you hear that voice?"

When Dingee said that he heard a loud voice in the distance, the Indians' spokesman laughed again and said, "That is Joseph's voice trying to persuade his young warriors not to kill you."[6] The voice must have come from Poker Joe, who would have been rousing the Indians to begin their travel day. Apparently, the Indians were teasing Dingee and playing on the similarity of the names of Poker Joe and Chief Joseph.

Arnold saw Dingee with the Indians and rushed to tell Frank Carpenter and Al Oldham to get up quickly.

Frank asked how many Indians there were.

"Three," Arnold said. He didn't know that more Indians were watching from the trees, and Poker Joe was camped down the Firehole River with most of the Nez Perce just a mile away. Chief Joseph's large Wallowa band was providing a rear guard, but they weren't far behind.

Frank wanted to find out the Indians' tribe. "What are they?" he asked.

"I don't know," Arnold replied, "but I think they are Nez Perce."

Frank told Arnold to wake everyone except Emma and Ida, but when he glanced at the tent, he saw Emma peeking out. She had already heard the strange voices and awakened George.

Frank rushed to the tent where he found Emma crying quietly.

Emma asked, "Is there danger?"

Frank replied, "I don't know; I hope not."

Frank told Emma to get George, and the men talked. They wanted to look for the chiefs and negotiate safe passage, but Emma begged them to keep the group together. To accommodate her, they decided to break camp and head down the Firehole River toward Henrys Lake. That route would take them directly through the main body of Indians who were streaming up the river.

Meanwhile, Yellow Wolf and his friends spotted the tourists' well-stocked supply wagon and demanded food. Arnold began to pass out flour and sugar from the tourists' still abundant supply, but when George saw what was happening, he rushed over and ordered the Indians away. His brusqueness probably diminished any possibility that the Indians would let the party go. As Emma put it in a reminiscence she wrote decades later, "I think this materially lessened his chance to escape."[7]

Emma said the tourists had shot up most of their ammunition hunting swans at Henrys Lake. She added it was "a fortunate thing probably that we had no more, for had the men been well armed, they would have attempted a defense, which could have only ended disastrously for us. Six men arrayed against several hundred Indians splendidly armed would not have survived long."[8]

Frank told Emma to keep herself and Ida hidden in the tent while he went to talk to the Indians.

"What is your name?" Frank asked one of the Indians.

"Me Charley," said the half-blood who spoke English, giving the name Indians often used when talking to strangers.[9]

"Where are the balance of the Indians?"

"Down there not far; camped on river down there," Charley answered, pointing down the Firehole River.

"Who chief?"

"Looking Glass, Joseph, White Bird, chiefs. Joseph, he toward the Henrys Lake about three days march." Charley named the chiefs of the largest Nez Perce bands instead of telling Frank that Poker Joe was in charge.

Frank asked if the Indians would kill the tourists.

"Don't know," Charley said, "maybe Injuns come steal horses, maybe kill. Don't know."

"Will chief kill citizens?"

"No, chief no kill you. No kill, you friends."

Frank asked if the tourists could wait at their camp in the Lower Geyser Basin until the Indians made their way up Nez Perce Creek and were gone.

"Don't know," Charley replied. "Maybe Joseph's Injuns come up here, kill you. Maybe want horses. Heap mad, Joseph's Injuns."[10]

"How many bad Indians?"

Charley replied by holding up both hands and spreading his fingers three times, meaning thirty.

Indians continued to arrive at the camp, and by the time the tourists were ready to leave forty or fifty armed men were escorting them. When the tourists crested a hill, they saw the main group of Indians. The six hundred fleeing Nez Perce didn't travel like soldiers passing a reviewing stand. Each of the five bands had its own camp composed of several lodges, and each lodge moved separately with its women, children, and men too old to fight. Young boys herded each lodge's horses and cattle, and warriors patrolled the areas around the herds.

Frank described the scene: "As far as we could see, up and down the river, they were moving in an unbroken line ten or fifteen feet deep, driving ponies and constantly riding out and in the line. We could see about three miles of Indians, with a thousand to fifteen-hundred ponies, and looking off to the left we could see more Indians looking at geysers in the Firehole Basin."[11]

When the tourists first started down the Firehole River toward Henrys Lake, they encountered many Indians who had left the main group to travel a mile out of their way to see the Lower Geyser Basin. The Indians' detour to view geysers belied assertions that they were afraid of them.

After traveling a couple of miles, the tourists ran into the main body of Indians, who were turning up Nez Perce Creek and heading over the Mary Mountain Pass toward the Yellowstone River.

The tourists continued down the Firehole River, passed through an open meadow, and approached a pine grove where their Indian escorts called a halt. One of the Indians raised his hand and shouted a command. In response to the summons, forty or fifty more Indians rode out of the timber where they had been waiting for the tourists.

Emma said, "Every Indian carried a splendid gun, with belts full of cartridges. As the morning sunshine glinted on the polished surface of the gun barrels, a regiment of soldiers could not have looked more formidable."[12]

The Indians, who were apparently messengers from Poker Joe, ordered the tourists to turn around and join him at the head of the Indians' column. Poker Joe must have feared that the tourists were headed directly toward hostile Indians who would kill them. Emma said, "The Indians pretended all the while to be our very good friends, saying that if they should let us go, bad Indians, as they termed them, would kill us."[13]

The travelers got back to the place where Nez Perce Creek ran into the Firehole River and turned up the trail toward Mary Mountain. Two miles farther along they came to a jumble of dead trees that had fallen across the trail and blocked their way, forcing them to abandon their wagons and proceed with only the few things they could carry on horseback.

As the campers rode away, Indians converged on their wagons and ransacked them. They turned the supply wagon upside down and tore apart the buggy wheels to take the spokes for whip handles. One Indian dashed past with several yards of mosquito netting tied to his horse's tail. Another wrapped a fine strip of swans down, a trophy collected at Henrys Lake, around his head like a turban.

Emma said, "We did not appreciate the fact that the Indians seemed to enjoy the 'confiscated property.'"[14] She commented that the Nez Perce were light-hearted and didn't seem worried about an attack from General Howard's men, whom they called "squaw soldiers." But she said they were watching for a group of eighty Bannock Indians led by a white scout named S. G. Fisher, whom the army had hired to find them.

While the tourists unhitched their wagons and saddled their horses, Frank decided to ride ahead to see if he could find the Indians' leader and negotiate safe passage.[15] About noon he reached the head of the Indian caravan, where he found Poker Joe camped for lunch with John Shively, the prospector the Indians had forced to be their guide. Frank told Poker Joe that he and his companions were just tourists and asked if they would be allowed to go home. Poker Joe said he would not harm civilians, but he would kill soldiers.

When the rest of the tourists arrived at Poker Joe's camp, he offered them a deal: if they would trade horses with the Indians, he would set them free. It was grossly unfair, but the tourists had little choice but to surrender their fine mounts for Indian horses that were worn out from hundreds of miles of hard travel.

Poker Joe took George's fine horse for himself, and several braves surrounded Emma, who was riding Bird, the beautiful white pony her father had given her. As Emma slipped out of the saddle, she was saddened by the thought that she would never see Bird again, but she was buoyed by the hope that she would soon be free. She said, "The Indians seemed friendly and the prospect of release probable."[16]

But the horse trading became rowdy with insolent Indians demanding the tourists' guns and knives. When the Indians began taking the tourists' clothing and blankets, Poker Joe saw he could no longer control his men, so he decided to send the tourists to hide in the timber.

Dingee said Poker Joe went to each member of the party, shook their hand, and told them to leave. Dingee paraphrased Poker Joe's admonition: "You had better get out of here the best way you can, if you want to save your lives. Get into the timber and don't go near the wagons. I wish you well, but have a number of young warriors who have lost relatives in battle and they are desperate. I cannot control them, and they are determined to kill you."[17]

When Poker Joe came to Arnold, he pointed to a large, gray horse standing near the woods and ordered Arnold to get it. When Arnold obeyed, Poker Joe went with him.

Poker Joe checked to see if the saddle was secure and said: "You get'm in woods. Stay in woods. No get'm on trail again. Go quick."[18] Then he shook Arnold's hand and shoved him toward the timber.

Arnold said that when he got into the brush he turned and saw Dingee walking backward and hiding beside a horse he was leading. Arnold saw an Indian, probably Poker Joe, with Dingee. Arnold thought the Indian was just waiting for others to start killing tourists, but he stopped, looked around, and told Dingee to join Arnold. Dingee headed for the trees. Arnold went with him.

The Indians had taken all the tourists' guns except for Al Oldham's Ballard rifle. Oldham had only three cartridges for the gun and they wouldn't fit any of the Indians' weapons, so they let him keep it. Poker Joe then ordered the remaining tourists to hide in the timber.

"Get'm horses quick," Poker Joe ordered. "Injuns come now. Bad Injuns come. They getting mad now. You go quick, my friends. You go out in timber. Keep in timber, my friends. No go out of woods."[19]

"Will we get away?" Frank asked.

"Yes, my friend," Poker Joe replied. "Me hope you get away, but Injuns heap mad."

Frank asked if the tourists could stay with Poker Joe, who apparently was trying to protect them.

"No," Poker Joe replied. "You go home now."

He then shook hands with each of the tourists. When he came to Emma and Ida, he said, "Good bye, my friends, good bye, my sisters."

Then Poker Joe mounted the beautiful horse he took from George, leaned over, and whispered to Frank: "My friend, go quick. Me tell you now go quick; bad Injuns over there." He pointed down Nez Perce Creek toward an open flat. Then he dug his heels in his horse's side and rode away up the creek toward the head of the column of Indians where the prospector, John Shively, was guiding them over Mary Mountain Pass.

The tourists headed into the timber, but they had gone only about thirty yards when they noticed Indians in twos and threes following them with guns cocked and ready to fire. Several other Indians approached and ordered the tourists out of the timber.

Then Charley asked, "Where balance of party?"[20]

"All here," Frank answered.

"No, two gone."

Frank looked around and confirmed that Arnold and Dingee had disappeared. "I sincerely thanked God," he recalled later. He was glad there would be survivors to tell the tourists' friends how they died.

Charley spoke to his Indian companions who started into the woods to find Dingee and Arnold. Then he turned to the tourists and said: "Two men get away. Injuns catch 'em now, kill 'em sure. No get away."

Frank asked Charley what would happen to the remaining tourists.

"You go home pretty soon," Charley replied. He said something to the Indians, and they made an opening so the tourists could go down the trail.

As the Indians sat still on their horses and the tourists started out, they heard two gunshots in the timber. The tourists assumed Dingee and Arnold were dead. The Indians yelled, and the tourists started again.

They rode along surrounded by Indians: George first, Ida next riding astride, and then Emma on her sidesaddle. Al Oldham followed Emma with his Ballard rifle in his hands.

The trail turned away from the open meadows along the creek and headed into thick timber. Then forty or fifty Indians came galloping toward the group. The Indians checked their horses, making them rear back. Two gunshots rang out.

The first bullet tore through Al Oldham's face, cutting through his tongue and coming out the right side of his jaw. Blood ran down his throat and over his vest.

Oldham tumbled from his horse, raised his rifle, and squeezed the trigger, but the gun misfired. He said later the gun's failure was fortunate. "Had I have shot him it would have been all up for the balance of the party."[21]

Oldham added, "It was lively times for the next few minutes, but during the time I kept my gun on the Indians, and they kept out of my way."[22] A commotion where George lay wounded drew the Indians' attention, and Oldham made for the brush and hid.

The second bullet hit George's leg. He felt a twinge in his thigh and slid from his horse. Emma screamed, dismounted, and ran to her husband. George started to run for cover in the bushes in a nearby ravine, but his gunshot leg was numb and he stumbled over a log. After he fell, he rolled over and leaned on a fallen pine.

Emma elbowed her way through the Indians and knelt beside her husband. "Oh, George," she said, "Where are you hurt?"[23]

George pointed to his right leg. Emma could see blood spurting out and feared the shot had severed an artery.

"What will they do with us?" she asked.

George and Emma Cowan returned to Yellowstone Park in 1901. They are shown with their family at the site of the couple's 1877 encounter with the Nez Perce.
GALLATIN HISTORY MUSEUM PHOTO

"Be brave, keep up, Emma," George replied. "If we have to die, we will go together."[24]

The Indians crowded around. Emma heard Ida screaming at the top of her lungs and rose to her knees. Ida kept screaming, so Emma stood up and summoned her. Ida arrived and calmed down. Every Indian pointed a gun at the trio: George, Emma, and Ida.

Emma said, "The holes in those gun barrels looked as big as saucers."[25]

The loss of blood gave George a raging thirst. He begged Emma to get him water, but she didn't dare leave him.

Emma felt a hand tugging on her shoulder. She turned and saw an Indian pointing a huge navy pistol at George's head. She jerked herself loose, grabbed the Indian's wrist, and shoved the gun aside.

"Kill me first,"[26] she yelled.

"No," the Indian replied, nodding at thirty-five-year-old George Cowan, "kill old one first."

The Indians began chanting from all sides: "Kill, kill, kill."

Then George turned his head and saw another Indian holding a revolver three inches from his face. He saw a flash and heard a blast. He heard Emma scream and felt a great weight crushing his head.

George's head jerked back and a red stream of blood trickled down his face. When Emma wrote about the scene decades later, she recalled these things: "The warm sunshine, the smell of blood, the horror of it all, a faint remembrance of seeing rocks thrown at his head, my sister's screams, a faint sick feeling, and all was black."[27]

John Shively was riding at the head of the Nez Perce caravan when he heard intermittent gunfire from the rear.[28] He assumed the shots meant death to all the Radersburg tourists and rode on.

CHAPTER 8

Joe Roberts's Adventure

Nineteen-year-old Joe Roberts was still living with his parents, so he needed his mother's permission to join a group of men going to Yellowstone Park in August 1877, but she was reluctant to let him go. No wonder. Mrs. Roberts doubtless had heard the news of Indians killing settlers and ferocious fights with soldiers in nearby Idaho Territory that had been appearing in Montana's territorial newspapers for weeks.

On June 21, *The Helena Weekly Herald* reported "serious trouble on the western border of this territory" between Nez Perce Indians and army units commanded by General O. O. Howard. The *Herald* noted the Nez Perce frequently came to Montana to hunt buffalo and were friends with several Montana tribes. According to the *Herald*, the Nez Perce could form alliances with the Sioux, Flathead, Bannock, or Crow Indians and attack Montana settlements.

"It is not our desire to produce unnecessary alarm among the people upon our western border," the *Herald* said, "but the situation is exceedingly serious, and people should be fully prepared for the worst that may come upon them."

On August 2, the *Herald* reported the Nez Perce had bypassed an earth-and-log barricade the army had thrown up at a narrow gap in the Lolo Pass west of Missoula to block the Indians from entering the Bitterroot Valley of Montana. The Indians had cut a deal with settlers and agreed to move peacefully up the Bitterroot Valley. Probably that was the news Mrs. Roberts had in mind when she and Richard Dietrich discussed the possibility of her son, Joe, going to Yellowstone Park with a group of Dietrich's friends. Professor Dietrich was a popular music teacher in Helena, so people liked and trusted him. Dietrich promised Mrs. Roberts that Joe would be safe—a promise that later cost Dietrich his life.

Dietrich might not have made that promise—and Mrs. Roberts might not have granted permission—had they known about the bloody battle between the Nez Perce and the army that began a hundred miles away on the banks of the Big Hole River on August 9. The Indians repulsed the army's predawn attack and fled, leaving behind ninety Nez Perce dead, most of them women and children. The army's atrocities shattered the Indians' agreement to pass through Montana settlements peacefully, and groups of young Nez Perce men began attacking ranches and stealing horses in the southwest corner of the territory. The main group of Nez Perce veered westward into Idaho and back east, where they raided General O. O. Howard's forces and made off with his pack mules. To avoid further confrontations with the army, they headed into Yellowstone Park.

On August 13, Professor Dietrich left Helena for the park with Joe Roberts, another boy named Fred Pfister, and another bachelor named Andrew Weikert. They made their way up the Missouri River Valley camping or getting permission to spend the night in ranchers' barns. Dietrich and his companions weren't worried about Indians as they passed through the settled areas. In fact, Roberts and Pfister were so boisterous that Weikert complained he had difficulty sleeping. About the only problem the travelers had was that their half-tame packhorses kept pulling their picket pins at night and wandering away.

Dietrich and his companions rode through Radersburg past the point where the Madison, Jefferson, and Gallatin rivers run together to form the Missouri. They crossed the smaller rivers and made their way to Bozeman on August 16. East of town they turned their horses out to graze and treated themselves to a home-cooked meal at the town's best hotel, but Weikert complained it was "a slim supper for hungry men."[1]

On August 18, after going over Trail Creek Pass between Bozeman and the Paradise Valley of the Yellowstone, they met the party of the famous Civil War general William Tecumseh Sherman, who was returning from a fifteen-day tour of the park. The general was rushing back to Fort Ellis to get more news about the bloody Big Hole Battle. Sherman had received newspapers and dispatches about the battle the day before, and he knew that his friend, Colonel John Gibbon, was injured and that other officers and men were killed. The Nez Perce had beaten back the army and escaped. Sherman and his companions wanted more news.

The meeting between Sherman's outgoing party and the incoming tourists lasted only about twenty minutes. The men gave Sherman copies of the latest newspapers that contained reports of Colonel Gibbon's casualties at the Big Hole—twenty-six killed and forty-two wounded—and of Gibbon's failure to capture the Nez Perce. Sherman's men reciprocated by sharing the information they had about the movements of the Indians. After giving the travelers suggestions for things to see in the park, the general hurried back to Fort Ellis for more news.[2]

Although they knew hostile Nez Perce were on the loose nearby, Roberts and his companions proceeded to Yellowstone Park. Perhaps they shared Sherman's view that Indians would not enter the park because they feared geysers.

Roberts and his friends arrived at Mammoth Hot Springs on the afternoon of August 20. They unpacked their horses and turned them loose to graze and rest up for the forthcoming trip through the park. Because they were staying to rest and see the sights at Mammoth for several days, they set up a more permanent camp than the ones they had while traveling from Helena. It was good that they pitched their tents because it rained that night.

There was a minor conflict when the music professor, Richard Dietrich, refused to share in camp chores like cooking and dish washing. A temporary agreement was that each member of the party would take care of his own cooking and dishes. Apparently, the feud ended when Ben Stone, an African American and professional cook, arrived and became the camp tender. In addition to the two men with Stone, Leander Duncan and Leslie Wilkie, another group of three arrived from Helena: Charles Kenck, Jack Stewart, and August Foller. In all the group, which came to be called the Helena Party, consisted of ten men.

While their horses rested, the men spent their time fishing in the nearby Gardner River and seeing the sights. They hiked up Mammoth Terraces and marveled at the multicolored pools and may have even taken baths in them.

The men got up bright and early on August 23 and were packed and ready to head farther into the park by 8 a.m. They arrived that afternoon at Tower Fall, where they stopped to admire the sights and have lunch. After camping overnight, the party made its way around Mount Washburn and arrived at Yellowstone Falls about 3 p.m. Everyone went to see the Upper Falls and had a beautiful sunset view of them. While some of the tourists returned to camp and staked the horses, others went fishing. Joe Roberts and Andrew Weikert took a walk to the Lower Falls. Weikert pronounced the view "glorious" and said anyone who didn't agree with that assessment "ought to be shut up in a dungeon and never see the light of day."[3] The group spent two full days at the falls fishing, admiring the views, and rolling rocks down the canyon.

The sun shone brightly on the morning of August 25 when the Helena Party left Yellowstone Falls for geyserland. Andy Weikert didn't want to leave the rumbling falls and the shining canyon, but he promised himself he would return someday.

When the men went to round up their horses, they discovered the one they called "Old Whitey" had sneaked away and hidden somewhere in the tall timber. After a quick search, the men decided it wasn't worth the effort to find the decrepit animal. Other horses could carry his share of the load because the packs were getting lighter. In fact, Weikert worried that food would run out before they finished their tour.

After packing, the men mounted and headed up a clear trail toward Sulphur Mountain eight miles away. Only seven years before, explorers didn't know the way from the falls to the grand geysers, but by 1877, the trail was well worn and easy to follow.

Several of the men had to stay with the packhorses to keep them from wandering off the trail and getting their bulging packs stuck between close-growing trees. But men who weren't needed to manage the packhorses roamed far and wide to hunt and see the sights. The party's route took them past Mud Volcano in a geothermal area of steam vents and erupting mud pots. The sulphur smell and unearthly sights there had reminded prospectors who visited them of hell.

The group stopped for lunch near Sulphur Mountain, where one of the men who had been roaming reported a moving caravan ahead. He thought it might be a herd of elk or buffalo, or maybe other tourists. Duncan took his spyglass and went up the mountain to see if he could figure out what the caravan was. He soon rushed back and announced: "There's a damned big party of tourists, or else a big band of elk ahead."[4]

Wilkie dismissed Duncan's claim that he had seen game. "Your elk," he said, "will turn out to be trees, like all that game you see."[5] The party continued forward, but the men got nervous when they kept seeing movement ahead. Some of the wanderers said they had seen moccasin tracks and the marks of unshod horses—sure signs that Indians were near.

Members of the Helena Party. Center photo from left: Joe Roberts, Richard Dietrich, and Fred Pfister. Upper left: Charles Kenck. Upper right: Richard Dietrich. Lower left: Leander Duncan. Lower right: Ben Stone.

"We could see something alive coming," Stone said. "We were all suspicious they were Indians, but thought they might be tourists."[6] Dietrich, Wilkie, and Kenck decided to spread out and reconnoiter. The remaining men traveled another mile and a half and crested a small hill where they saw a large Indian camp across the Yellowstone River.

"Indians! Indians!" Duncan exclaimed. "My God, it's Indians."[7] He wanted to turn around immediately, but others talked him into waiting for the scouts to report. Kenck was the first scout to return and said he saw three hundred Indians camped across the Yellowstone River. Dietrich came in next with the same report, which was greeted as "old news." Then Wilkie returned and confirmed the others' reports.

The men held what Weikert called a "council of war." Some thought the Indians probably were friendly and would cause no harm. But others thought they might be hostile Nez Perce. If the Indians were friendly, the men figured, there was no reason for concern, but if they were the Nez Perce, it would be prudent to "advance to the rear." After all, the Indians outnumbered the travelers sixty to one.

Perhaps motivated by thoughts of his wife and infant daughter and a premonition that he would die soon, Kenck got off his horse, tightened the cinch on his saddle, remounted, and announced he was going to ride back as fast as he could. He then galloped up the trail. The others followed as fast as they could, but the packhorses slowed them down. Kenck soon disappeared in the distance.

The packhorses' saddles swayed as they rushed along, loosening their cinches. Stewart, Weikert, and Dietrich stayed behind to secure the packs. When the main group got too far ahead, Roberts doubled back to find the men working on the packs. After the group reassembled, they decided to send Weikert to find a campsite where they could hide until the Indians passed.

Weikert rode to a point above Yellowstone Falls where Otter Creek ran into the Yellowstone River. He headed a mile and a half up the creek to a spot where it forked. Between the forks was a perfect hiding place on a high ridge with an open meadow to provide grazing for the horses and timber to provide firewood and places to hide.[8]

The men posted a guard, gathered wood, built a fire, and prepared supper. After the men ate, they argued about whether the Indians were hostile. Some thought they were probably friendly Indians from nearby reservations, either

Crow from the north or Bannocks from the west. Others said they must be the Nez Perce because they seemed to be rushing like the army was chasing them.

Finally, the men decided to send their most experienced outdoorsmen, Weikert and Wilkie, out the next day to see if the Indians had moved on. If the Indian camp was gone, they figured, the danger would be over. But they were wrong. They didn't know that the Indians always had groups of scouts out in all directions from their main group to reconnoiter and round up any horses they could find. And those groups of a dozen or more scouts still were enraged by the army's sneak attack at the Big Hole. They were looking for revenge.

After dark, Charles Kenck arrived at the camp. He had fled as far as the party's campsite at the Yellowstone Falls and rested there. When nobody caught up with him, he decided to hang a note conspicuously in a tree saying he was going on to Mammoth Hot Springs. But then he must have thought traveling alone the forty miles from the falls to the hot springs was too dangerous and made a fatal decision to turn back and rejoin his friends.

When the men asked Kenck how he found their camp, he said he saw smoke from their fire. That disturbed the men, who thought they had been careful about staying hidden. If Kenck could find their camp, Indians could too.

The group kept a guard posted until 10 o'clock, but with no activity in sight, they lay down to sleep in their blankets. They kept their clothes on—and their guns handy. Duncan was so frightened that he took his blankets and made his bed a half-mile away in the woods. Weikert said he didn't close his eyes the whole night.

The next morning, Weikert and Wilkie left to reconnoiter, and the rest of the travelers lolled around the camp telling jokes and napping. They didn't post guards apparently because they felt safe in their camp hidden under a hill between a grove of thick timber and a small creek that ran into the Yellowstone River. Besides, Weikert and Wilkie had said they would fire rifle shots as a warning if they saw hostile Indians.

The camp cook, Ben Stone, joked with his companions to cheer them up. He said he would bake bread and wash the dishes so if the Indians arrived they would find something good to eat and clean dishes to eat off of. Leander Duncan was especially downhearted, so Stone told him he should be thinking about a girl to marry—not about Indians. Everybody laughed at that.

Then rifle shots rang out.

Jack Stewart was asleep when the Indians attacked. When he heard the gunshots and war whoops he rose up and saw Indians fifteen feet away. He jumped up and ran through the brush. He came to a small park where he saw Charles Kenck a hundred feet ahead. As Stewart ran, he felt a bullet pierce his leg and heard Charles Kenck yell, "Oh my God." Stewart kept running, but another bullet hit him in the hip and knocked him down. Two Indians ran by, and Stewart heard two more shots. Then he heard Kenck crying out, "I'm murdered."[9] Kenck was shot twice. One bullet pierced his body and another broke his neck.

While one Indian plundered Kenck's body, another shoved a gun in Stewart's face. He threw up his hands and begged for his life. The Indian demanded to know if Stewart had any money. After he confessed he did, the Indian pulled $263 and a silver watch from his breast pocket. The Indian inspected Stewart's wounds, declared they probably wouldn't kill him, and walked away.

Fred Pfister was away from camp gathering wood when he heard the Indians' guns and war whoops. He looked back and saw his companions scattering as the Indians entered the camp. He jumped the creek and dashed toward the river. When he reached the bank, he looked back and heard someone yell, "Oh, my God!" Then he headed toward McCartney's cabin at Mammoth Hot Springs.

The music professor, Richard Dietrich, tried to jump the creek but fell in. He hunkered down in a deep spot and hid. The tall grass on the banks kept the Indians from seeing him. Dietrich waited in the cold water for four hours. After the Indians left, he started walking to Mammoth. Duncan hid in the brush until dark and also made his way to Mammoth Hot Springs.

When the Indians attacked, their rifle shots and war whoops awakened Joe Roberts. At first Joe thought that Weikert and Wilkie were making a racket to scare everybody for fun. But when he jumped to his feet, he saw an Indian with an ugly scar running across his cheek under his left eye. The Indian, who was just twenty feet away, held a lever-action Winchester rifle.

Roberts turned away, ran down the hill, and jumped the creek. As he ran up the hill on the other side, Joe heard rifle bullets whizzing past as the Indian emptied the Winchester's magazine. He saw Duncan and Kenck reach the timber under heavy fire.

When Roberts reached dense timber, he heard August Foller call for him to wait—and he did. The two men caught their breath; then they ran deeper into the timber. After traveling more than a mile, they sat down to rest again. Then they began walking—southward away from Mammoth Hot Springs and deeper into the Yellowstone wilderness.

Staying out of sight in the timber, the boys began to move again. Unlike the rest of the party, they fled to the south—away from Mammoth Hot Springs. When darkness fell they laid down by a big log to sleep. Roberts didn't have a coat, so Foller took the outside.

The awoke at sunrise and headed northwest looking for the Madison River. They continued all day without food except for a few wild berries plucked from bushes as they moved along. They spent another cold night in the timber.

The next day Roberts and Foller crossed the divide separating the Yellowstone drainage from the Madison and made their way down a dry gulch. They came to a small stream and finally to the Madison River where they found a small cabin, where they stopped to rest and ease their blistered feet.

Foller dug a fishing line out of his pocket and caught three fish, which they roasted over a fire. They ate two of the fish but saved the third for later. Then the continued their march, making their beds that night in tall grass by the river.

After traveling several miles the next morning, Roberts and Foller sat down to eat their last fish, then continued their journey. As they came around a bend in the river about noon, they spotted several men on the other side. They were teamsters transporting supplies to General Howard's army, which was bivouacked at Henrys Lake.

One of the teamsters rode across the river leading two horses to rescue the pair. Back at their wagons, the teamsters gave each of them a dram of whisky and made them eat slowly. They provided supplies—canned salmon, tomatoes, hardtack, and a loaf of bread—and gave them directions to Virginia City. Roberts and Foller proceeded, still on foot, staying that night in a deserted house.

About noon the next day they met a man looking for lost horses. The man sent the lost men to his wagon while he rounded up the horses. Then he took them to Virginia City, where they caught the next stagecoach back to Helena, arriving there on September 1. Back at his mother's house, Joe nursed his blistered feet and told his story to newspaper reporters.

CHAPTER 9

A Decent Burial

Three bachelors were willing to risk their lives for the men who fled into the Yellowstone wilderness after the Nez Perce attacked the Helena Party in August 1877. Ben Stone, the African American cook and party's camp tender, was the oldest person in the group at age forty-four, but his race apparently kept him from getting much respect. Even the youngest members of the party felt free to tease Stone, but that didn't bother the amiable cook, who returned their gibes in a heavy southern accent. Stone accepted his status and his job of taking care of the younger men in his charge—and not just by feeding them.

Richard Dietrich was just twenty-four when he joined the party, but he had already made himself an important part of the social scene in Helena. Professor Dietrich was a music teacher who had emigrated from Prussia and began teaching music at the Montana territorial capital. Dietrich was not only the organist and choirmaster for Saint Peter's Episcopal Church, he was also the leader of the Helena Silver Coronet Band and the founder of the Gesang Verein Harmonica Choir. Through these organizations, Dietrich provided music for concerts, weddings, and all sorts of celebrations. He also taught music to children in Helena's best homes, and he promised their parents he would watch over those who went on the Yellowstone Park adventure.

At the age of thirty-one, Andrew Weikert was already a seasoned outdoorsman whose expertise made him a de facto leader of the Helena Party. Weikert operated his own mining claim north of Helena, and he knew how to ride a horse and shoot a gun. He was ready to use those skills to protect his companions from hostile Indians.

Weikert didn't close his eyes the night after the Helena Party went into hiding when they saw the Nez Perce crossing the Yellowstone River. He got up and ate breakfast on the peaceful morning of August 26 and felt better. He figured if the Indians were going to attack the travelers—"whoop them up"[1] as he put it—they would have done so during the night. He decided to ride

Members of the Helena Party of ten tourists that Nez Perce scouts attacked on August 26, 1877, killing one and scattering the rest into the wilderness. From left: Joe Roberts, Andrew Weikert, and Fred Pfister.
MONTANA HISTORICAL SOCIETY PHOTO

back to the Yellowstone River to see if the Indians had moved on. If they had, he figured it would be safe for him and his companions to continue their trip. Leslie Wilkie, a thirty-year-old clerk for the Montana Surveyor General's office, agreed to go scouting with Weikert.

When Weikert and Wilkie got to the place where they had seen the Nez Perce crossing the Yellowstone River the day before, there were no Indians in sight. It looked like the danger had passed, so they turned back to tell their companions the coast was clear and that they could continue their trip to Lake Yellowstone. They would then backtrack to Mary Mountain Pass and go on to the grand geysers. Weikert and Wilkie hurried so there would be time enough for the group to get to Lake Yellowstone that evening. When they got two miles from where their companions' camp was hidden on Otter Creek, they saw an Indian pony near the trail and decided to catch it. Weikert roped the pony, but it wasn't broken to lead and wouldn't follow. The men tried to drive the animal, but it refused to go in the right direction. Finally, they decided the horse wasn't worth the effort. Weikert choked it down to retrieve his rope and let it go. The time the men lost trying to capture the horse may have had fatal consequences.

Weikert and Wilkie rode straight into an ambush. They got within a hundred feet before they saw the Indians hiding behind a log under a hill. Weikert said the sight "made our hair raise and the blood rush to our faces."[2]

When Weikert saw an Indian raise his head above the log, he wheeled his horse, warned Wilkie, and raised his gun. Looking back, he saw six rifles pointed at him, so he scrunched down to make himself small. The Indians fired and bullets zipped past.

Weikert recalled, "I was perfectly cool and self-possessed, but will own up that my hair was standing on end."[3] Weikert's horse jumped, and the Indians fired again. The second volley was more successful; a bullet cut a four-inch gash in Weikert's shoulder blade. Weikert said the bullet "splintered my shoulder a little bit"[4] but didn't break a bone. Another bullet knocked a piece of wood off the stock of his rifle.

Weikert hugged his horse even tighter and raced away. The Indians fired again, but he was out of range. He heard the bullets fly and hit the trees. He feared the Indians would mount their horses and give chase. Weikert's horse stumbled and fell, almost turning a somersault, and he went spiraling. He thought his horse had been shot, but when he stood up he discovered he had the reins in one hand and his rifle in the other.

Although his wounded shoulder hurt, he knew he had to get away because he could see the Indians running toward him to get close enough for another shot. He figured his only chance was "to get behind a tree and turn my old repeater loose on the redskins."[5] Then he saw another opportunity; his horse had stood up.

Weikert said, "I up and let them have one with my repeater, and you ought to have seen them dodge."[6] He grabbed the saddle horn, bounded into the saddle, and raced away. As he turned back to take another shot at the Indians, he brushed close to a tree and a limb knocked his hat off. He abandoned the hat and raced on. When he looked back, he saw the Indians standing with their mouths open, apparently surprised at the speed of his escape.

Weikert caught up with Wilkie, and the men rode into the timber. The Indians wouldn't follow them there because it was easy for a man to hide in the brush and ambush a pursuer. When the brush got too thick for the men to ride, they got off their horses and started walking. When they finally stopped to catch their breath, Wilkie asked Weikert if he was hurt. Weikert said judging by the hole in his shirt and the blood running into his boot, he must at least have been scratched.

Wilkie examined Weikert's wounded shoulder and dressed it as well as he could. The men examined their horses and found the animals sound, so they mounted and rode away as fast as they could. They hoped to get to the camp and warn their companions about the hostile Indians.

They stuck to the timber and skirted around a small mountain to avoid being seen. When they got close to the camp, they shouted out, but no answer came back. They rode into the deserted camp and found bedding and camp equipment smoldering in the campfire and shotguns that the Indians didn't want smashed against the trees. The horses were gone—all fourteen of them.

After a quick search for their companions—either bodies or alive and in hiding—Weikert and Wilkie found a ham and some other food scattered around and shoved it into their saddlebags. Then they left for Mammoth Hot Springs. The men rode in the timber to keep from being seen and moved slowly. Their horses were exhausted, and the Springs were fifty miles away. They wouldn't get there until morning anyway.

As they rode along, they spied two men moving slowly in the distance ahead. One of those men hobbled along, supporting himself with a stick; the other rode a horse bareback. Weikert took out his field glasses and determined the men weren't Indians. Weikert and Wilkie rushed to catch up with them.

They were Jack Stewart and the camp cook, Ben Stone. Stewart had been shot twice, once in the back of his leg above his ankle and once where a rifle ball had hit him in the back and passed through his hip bone.

Stewart's injuries were so severe that he couldn't ride a horse bareback except on level ground, and hilly country lay between him and Mammoth Hot Springs. But when Stewart was put on Wilkie's horse he could brace his legs in the stirrups and ride over rough country. With Stewart on Wilkie's horse and Stone on Weikert's, the quartet resumed their trek. Weikert and Wilkie traded riding bareback on Stewart's mare.

As the men climbed the trail up Mount Washburn, Stewart said he felt faint and had to dismount and rest for a couple of hours. But Weikert wouldn't let the group stop because he feared that if they did, they wouldn't start again until the next day. He walked beside Stewart and offered reassurance, although his own shoulder wound ached badly.

At the top of Mount Washburn, the men stopped to eat some ham and crackers from their saddlebags. That revived Stewart enough to go on.

Ben Stone's horse was exhausted after being ridden fifteen hours, and it began to fall behind. Stone was scared he would be left, so he asked Weikert to follow him. Weikert complied.

As they approached the Hot Springs, they met a man who was rushing to the Clarks Fork Mines on the northeast edge of the park to warn that Indians were coming. The man told the travelers that the army had already brought their companion, Fred Pfister, to McCartney's cabin along with Emma Cowan and Frank and Ida Carpenter of the Radersburg Party. The flamboyant showman and guide, Texas Jack Omohundro, and the two Englishmen he had been guiding through the park, also were already at McCartney's.

Andy Weikert and his battered entourage rode up to McCartney's cabin at Mammoth Hot Springs about six in the morning. Although Weikert had been awake for forty-eight hours, he couldn't sleep. It wasn't just the four-inch bullet gash across his shoulder blade that kept him awake. Weikert was worried about his missing companions.

While Weikert fretted, Leander Duncan arrived from the wilderness and reported that Richard Dietrich had collapsed at the Gardner River about two miles from the cabin. Weikert immediately saddled two horses and hurried away to retrieve the popular music teacher.

When he found the exhausted Dietrich lying beside the trail, the music teacher greeted him, "Oh Andy, let me ride one of those horses for I cannot walk any farther."[7]

When Weikert explained that he had come to help, Dietrich was profuse with thanks and praise. He explained that he was exhausted because he had hidden in cold water for eight hours to avoid attacking Indians. Weikert told him the time in the water was probably less than half that.

"All right," Dietrich conceded, "but indeed it seemed that long to me."[8]

Weikert helped Dietrich onto a horse and led him back to McCartney's cabin. When the music teacher dismounted he couldn't stand, but a few good soaks in the baths at McCartney's revived him.

Weikert turned his horse loose to graze and waited until the next day for more of his companions to return. When nobody arrived by noon, he saddled his horse again and rode eight miles to a vista where he could see for another four miles. He scanned the area with his field glasses but saw no sign of his missing friends.

In a reminiscence he wrote years later, Weikert said, "I returned sad at heart but with a determination to go back and hunt for them if I could persuade someone to go with me."[9]

Weikert waited until the next morning, but nobody volunteered. Wilkie had ridden back to Bozeman with the army to summon an ambulance to rescue Stewart, and a freight wagon had already left for Bozeman with Emma Cowan and her sister, Ida Carpenter, plus most of the able-bodied men.

Weikert decided to go back to the wilderness alone that evening, but Jim McCartney talked him out of that. McCartney said he would go with Weikert, but only if they could wait until the next morning. Although Weikert thought he had already waited too long and was willing to travel through the night, he decided to accept McCartney's plan.

Weikert and McCartney begged Dietrich to go to Bozeman on the ambulance that was coming for Stewart, but the music teacher wouldn't do that. He said he had to wait because he promised to look after Joe Roberts. With tears in his eyes, Dietrich said, "What will Mrs. Roberts say if I go and leave Joe? What shall I say when I meet his mother, when she asks me where Joe is?"[10]

McCartney joked about the Indians coming to scalp everybody and told Dietrich he should look out for his hair. The music professor replied he would try, then he turned to Weikert and said, "Andy, you will give me a decent burial, won't you?"[11]

Weikert later said, "I told him jestingly that I would, never thinking that I would be called on to perform the reality so soon. How little I thought it would be the last time I would see him alive."[12]

Weikert and McCartney started into the wilderness with two saddle horses and two packhorses. They crossed the Gardner River and traveled along Lava Creek through hilly country past Undine Falls. Then they turned south until they intercepted Tower Creek, crossed over Mount Washburn, and hurried past the Yellowstone Falls.

As Weikert and McCartney rode along, they kept their eyes out for signs of the Nez Perce, but they weren't vigilant enough. They must have ridden past a group of eighteen Indians who were on their way to steal horses at Henderson's Ranch, which was past Mammoth Hot Springs seven miles north of the park.

After riding hard for forty miles, Weikert and McCartney decided to stop for the night about ten miles from their goal, the spot on Otter Creek where the Nez Perce had attacked the Helena Party four days before.

The next morning Weikert and McCartney rode up Otter Creek to the old campsite and began their search for the missing members of the Helena Party. They found Charles Kenck's body about three hundred yards from the campsite. Kenck had been shot in the back of the head with the rifle ball exiting beside his nose. Another shot had hit him in the back. The attackers had rifled his body, but they missed a silver watch in his pocket.

Weikert and Wilkie buried Kenck and spent the rest of the day searching in the trees and along the creek banks for the missing men, Joe Roberts and August Foller. Finally, they decided Roberts and Foller must have escaped, so they packed up everything that could be recovered at the camp and returned to the spot where they had stayed the night before.

After Weikert and McCartney fixed supper and made their beds, they went to picket their horses so they would not wander away overnight. McCartney became nervous and said to Weikert, "Andy, something tells me we had better go on."[13]

Weikert agreed, so the men packed up, saddled their horses, and left. As they rode away, Weikert looked back and saw an Indian ride across an opening in the timber. He figured the Indian wanted to find out "how we were fixed."[14] The men rode twenty miles until about 3 a.m. and then stopped to rest. They turned their spent horses out to graze.

When the men woke the next morning, the horses were gone, and they began a search. They were beginning to think Indians had stolen the horses when they finally found them about 9 o'clock. They saddled and packed their horses and started toward Mammoth Hot Springs, which was still eighteen miles away.

That afternoon Weikert and McCartney reached a wide valley bordered by aspen groves and thick underbrush. There they saw eighteen Indians riding toward them two hundred yards ahead. They turned their horses and galloped toward the nearest brush.

Weikert later recalled, "Eighteen guns kept up quite a racket and they got some balls pretty close. We could hear the balls whistle through the air and see them pick up the dust. We returned fire as best we could and think we made some good Indians."[15] ("Good Indians" was a reference to a comment attributed to General Philip Sheridan: "The only good Indian is a dead Indian.")

The men angled toward the timber together for a while. Then McCartney pointed his horse straight up the hill while Weikert continued along a gentler slope. The Indians dismounted and took cover behind a pile of rocks. "They kept pouring lead into the hill close around me,"[16] Weikert said. They were only two hundred yards away.

A rifle ball hit Weikert's horse, and the animal stopped short. When Weikert dismounted he saw blood running out of the horse's side. He told the doomed animal, "Goodbye, Toby. I have not time to stay but must make the rest of the way afoot."[17]

McCartney's frightened horse bucked him off and the saddle turned under its belly. Weikert saw what was happening, pulled his knife, and tried to catch the horse to cut the saddle off, but the animal dashed away.

Indian rifle balls kicked up dust around Weikert. He estimated the Indians fired fifty times but succeeded only in killing his horse and cutting a piece from his boot leg.

The men dashed to a fallen log and hid behind it. McCartney wanted to stay there, but Weikert thought the log didn't provide enough cover and said he was making for the brush.

McCartney was wearing spurs that would keep him from running, so he asked Weikert to wait. McCartney put his hand on his companion's shoulder and jerked off his spurs. He threw them under the log, saying he might return for them later. Then the men ran to the brush and the Indians laid down a barrage of gunfire.

The Indians didn't follow the men into the thicket where they could return fire from under cover. As Weikert put it, "They were terrible brave so long as they had the advantage, but just as soon as the tables were turned, they made themselves scarce in the hills."[18]

The men hid for an hour. Then they ventured out to see if the Indians had gone and if they could find their horses. They saw Indians four miles away but couldn't locate any horses, so they started for Mammoth Hot Springs on foot.

When they came to the Gardner River, they had to take off their clothes and hold them over their heads while they waded across the rushing water. Darkness had fallen by the time they got across and dressed. They were still two miles from McCartney's cabin.

When the men finally arrived at the cabin, they saw the door standing open. Fearing they might be taken for Indians in the darkness, they called out, but there was no answer.

They entered the cabin, found a candle on the table, and lit it with a match. Then they turned and saw Richard Dietrich's body on the floor. They searched for other bodies, but when they didn't find any they concluded that Ben Stone, John Stewart, and the teamster, Stoner, had gotten away.

Weikert was exhausted from hard travel and lack of sleep, and his wounded shoulder was aching. McCartney searched the cabin for food, but when he couldn't find anything, he decided they should go on to Henderson's Ranch, which was seven miles to the north.

When the men saw fresh horse tracks in the road, they decided there must be Indians ahead, so they kept a sharp lookout. Whenever they heard a noise, they rushed into the brush and hid. The sounds they heard must have come from Ben Stone, who had escaped the Indians at Mammoth Hot Springs and was also on his way to Henderson's.

Finally, Weikert was so exhausted that he asked McCartney to stop and let him sleep. Weikert said that after McCartney acceded to his request, "I flopped myself down behind the sagebrush, where I had hardly hit the ground til I was fast asleep."[19] McCartney kept watch while Weikert slept.

After a couple of hours, Weikert awoke and the men soon were on the road again. As they approached Henderson's Ranch, they heard a cowbell and joked that they could get some milk if nothing else.

Then they saw a man rise up in the darkness from the sagebrush. Weikert and McCartney dropped to their knees and raised their guns to shoot. But a guard called out, "Who goes there?" Recognizing the voice as a white man's, the men replied, "Friends."

Weikert and McCartney entered the camp of Lieutenant Gustavus C. Doane, who had been sent to keep the Nez Perce from leaving the park down the Yellowstone River. Doane and his cavalrymen, along with a contingent

McCartney's cabin at Mammoth Hot Springs provided shelter to members of the Helena and Radersburg parties fleeing the park. Nez Perce scouts killed Richard Dietrich there.

NATIONAL PARK SERVICE PHOTO

of Crow Indians, had seen smoke rising earlier that afternoon and rushed to Henderson's Ranch to find it in flames. Nez Perce scouts had attacked the ranch, driven its occupants into the hills, set buildings afire, and then fled with the ranch horses. Apparently, they were the same Indians who had attacked Weikert and Wilkie earlier that day.

A young officer with Doane, Lieutenant Hugh Lenox Scott, with ten troops pursued the Indians to Mammoth Hot Springs. Scott said, "We rounded a point and at McCartney's cabin in a side gulch found a white man lying dead at the door, not yet cold. He had been standing in the doorway, looking out, when one of the Indians we were chasing rounded the point and shot him."[20] The dead man was Richard Dietrich.

Apparently, Scott's assumption that the Indians he was chasing killed Dietrich was wrong. Yellow Wolf told a different story decades later. Yellow Wolf said he was traveling with a different party of young Nez Perce and one of his companions killed Dietrich. Yellow Wolf recalled it was about sunset when his party arrived at Mammoth. Yellow Wolf said his group of six or seven men saw a man standing in the doorway of a house. One of Yellow Wolf's companions said three of his brothers and a sister, who were not warriors, were killed at the Big Hole.

"It was just like this man that did that killing of my brothers and sister," the companion said. "He is nothing but a killer to become a soldier sometime. We are going to kill him now."[21]

Then the companion raised his rifle and fired, hitting Dietrich in the arm. Then another man fired, killing Dietrich.

Lieutenant Scott led his men past the Liberty Cap and found the fleeing Indians' trail, but he feared an ambush if he followed it. He returned to Lieutenant Doane's camp at Henderson's Ranch. It was the tracks of Scott and his men that Weikert and McCartney had seen when they made their way to the ranch.

When Weikert and McCartney arrived at Doane's camp, Ben Stone recognized their voices. Stone jumped up, grabbed Weikert's hand, and said, "God bless you, Andy. I never expected to see you any more."[22] Stone broke into tears as he recounted the Indians' attack at Mammoth Hot Springs and his escape.

The next day, Weikert returned to Mammoth Hot Springs with several citizens and soldiers to bury Dietrich. They couldn't find lumber to make a casket, so they buried the body in an old bathtub. Then they returned to Doane's camp.

Weikert still felt responsible for the missing men, Joe Roberts and August Foller, but he headed back to Bozeman to get new clothing and fresh horses. He planned to return to the park and search until he found the missing men, but five miles from Bozeman he met a man who told him they had arrived in Virginia City three days before. Weikert rushed to Bozeman to get details. He learned that Roberts and Foller had fled southward through the park when the Indians attacked. They survived their three-day trek eating only wild berries and three little fishes. By the time Weikert reached Bozeman, Roberts and Foller had taken the stagecoach back to Helena.

Weikert also went back home to Helena to rest and give his wounded shoulder a chance to heal. But he didn't forget his promise to give Richard Dietrich a proper burial. Seven weeks later on October 11 he headed back to Yellowstone Park to recover the bodies of Dietrich and Charles Kenck. He

Richard Dietrich, a popular music teacher from Helena, escaped the Indian attack near Yellowstone Falls on August 26, 1877. Nez Perce scouts killed him at Mammoth Hot Springs a few days later.

MONTANA HISTORICAL SOCIETY PHOTO

got back to Helena two weeks later with Dietrich's remains, but deep snow had already blocked the trail over Mount Washburn, so Weikert couldn't get back to the campsite where the Indians had killed Kenck. He asked James McCartney to retrieve Kenck's body as soon as the route became passable the next spring.

Weikert took Dietrich's body to Gesang Verein, the harmonica music society the professor had helped establish. The society bought a casket and held a funeral for their beloved teacher on October 28.

After Weikert fulfilled his promise to make sure Dietrich got a proper burial, he resumed work on his mine claim in Dry Gulch north of Helena.

CHAPTER 10
Captivity and Release

Emma Cowan had fainted when she saw an Indian shoot her husband, George, in the head with a heavy navy pistol. When she started to regain her senses, Emma heard a jumble of noises—hooting, yelling, neighing of horses, and someone calling her name through the din. When she came to fully, she saw her brother, Frank Carpenter, close by. He tried to comfort his ashen-faced sister by telling her the Indians had promised they wouldn't be harmed further. Emma wasn't reassured.

"I could see nothing," she said, "but my husband's dead face with blood upon it."[1] She recalled later that Frank told her that their thirteen-year-old sister, Ida, was safe, but Emma didn't react to the news at the time.

The Indians soon discovered that Frank recently had been over the Mary Mountain trail that led from the Madison drainage to the Yellowstone River, so they ordered him ahead to the front of the column to guide the way.

The narrow trail was wide enough for small tourist groups, but six hundred Indians and their 1,500 horses were trying to pass through the thick stands of lodgepole pine. Loose horses sometimes strayed into the timber and were lost. Mules loaded with wide packs sometimes got stuck between close-standing trees. When that happened, Indian women beat the animals in the head until they lurched backward and freed themselves.

The group that Emma traveled with continued climbing through the thick forest until they reached the summit. As they headed down, the timber thinned into open glades and parks. At dusk the travelers came to Hayden Valley, which had already begun to glow with campfires. The Indian who led Emma's horse threaded his way past several camps and finally stopped near one of them.

At another camp the Indians had put Frank to work at camp chores like gathering firewood and starting a fire. An Indian woman handed him a coffee pot and a brass kettle and ordered him to fetch water. When he headed toward a stream, a man demanded to know where he was going. After Frank explained, the man told him if the Indians saw he was a white man he would be killed "for sure." The man then wrapped a blanket around Frank and told him to cover his head with it. "You Injun now,"[2] he said, walking with Frank to the stream.

Frank held the blanket close to his face but kept his eye peeled, looking for his sisters. While he was dipping water from the stream, he asked his companion where his sisters were. The companion said Ida was at another camp but he didn't know where Emma was.

When Frank returned to camp with water, he tossed the blanket on the ground but was ordered to put it back on, covering his head, and to sit down far from the campfire light where his face couldn't be seen. Frank watched the Indians setting up camp and thought about the day's events: "of the death of the boys whom I knew so well and regarded so highly, of the terrible fate of my sisters, and the inevitable death, as I supposed, in store for me."[3]

Frank contemplated his dismal situation. "I thought of our happiness of the night before when we were all together, full of bright anticipations of a pleasant journey home and compared it with our present situation. Then so full of life, now six of the boys lying, mangled in the woods, cold in death.

"I thought, too, of the pleasant home circle. They, having heard of the Indian war, would certainly be solicitous as to our welfare. They would hear of our tragic fate, but what a horrible revelation our bleaching bones would make."

As Frank sat brooding over his fate, he looked up and saw Emma arriving on a pony. He jumped up and rushed to meet her, but when he extended his hand she stepped back. Then he threw back the blanket and said, "Emma, don't you know me?"[4]

In her recollection of the event, Emma said, "Until he spoke I thought it to be an Indian, and I was clasped in the arms of my brother."[5] Frank led Emma to a campfire where a silent Indian sat. The man, who Emma later learned was Chief Joseph, motioned for Emma to sit. Emma said Frank tried to talk with Chief Joseph but without avail.

"The chief sat by the fire, sombre and silent," Emma recalled, "foreseeing in his gloomy meditations possibly the unhappy ending of his campaign. The 'noble red man' we read about was more nearly impersonated in this Indian than any I have ever met. Grave and dignified, he looked a chief."[6]

Emma said Frank tried to conciliate the Indians by taking a baby from an Indian woman and placing it in her lap. "I glanced at the chief and saw the glimmer of a smile on his face, showing he had a heart beneath the stony exterior."[7]

The Indian woman smiled but saw that Emma was crying and asked Frank, "Why cry?" He told her Emma's husband had been killed. "She heartsick," the Indian woman said.

"I was indeed," Emma recalled.

Emma asked the Indian women who were preparing supper where her sister, Ida, was. They told her that the thirteen-year-old was at the camp of Poker Joe, who was in charge of the combined bands of the Nez Perce then. They also said Poker Joe was holding John Shively, the prospector who Emma and her friends had met at the Upper Geyser Basin the day before.

Emma and Frank spent their first night of captivity sitting next to the dying embers of a campfire. Frank said the Indians told him they would be set free the next day, but Emma doubted that. She remembered that the day before, one group of Indians said the tourists could go home, but then another group shot her husband and drove the other men into the wilderness before capturing her, Ida, and Frank.

As the morning of August 25 approached, rain began to fall. An Indian woman got up and replenished the fire and spread a piece of canvas over Emma's shoulders to keep her dry. At dawn, the Indian woman restarted the campfire and prepared breakfast. She offered some soda bread and willow tea, but Emma couldn't eat.

Poker Joe arrived and offered to take Emma to her sister, but he told Frank to remain in camp. As she departed, Emma clasped Frank's hand, wondering if she would ever see him again.

After a short walk—one she would gladly have taken the night before—Emma found Ida. Emma recounted the reunion like this: "Such a forlorn child I trust I may never again see. She threw herself into my arms in a very paroxysm of joy. She seemed not to be quite certain that I was alive."[8]

In her account of the events of the day before, Ida recalled when the Indians took her and her siblings captive. She said she jumped from her horse and ran to be near her sister and brother-in-law, Emma, and George Cowan.

"I was so terrified I could scarcely walk," Ida said. "I was benumbed all over, and the froth from my mouth was like paste. I thought certainly I was soon going to be killed."[9]

Ida saw Emma kneeling next to George with her arms around his neck, when one Indian pulled her away and another pointed a revolver at his head and fired. Emma fainted. Ida screamed.

Ida tried to escape by darting in and out among the Indians' horses, but an Indian grabbed her by the throat. He choked her, leaving bruises that lasted for two weeks. Ida said when the Indian loosened his grip she "had the satisfaction of biting his fingers."[10] The Indians put Ida on a horse behind one of the men. As the pair rode away, Ida could see Emma mounted behind an Indian ahead of her. She thought the Indians had killed Frank.

Ida thought about her family waiting back in Radersburg. She recalled her parents kissing her goodbye, and her fifteen-year-old brother, Willie, waving farewell with a handkerchief from the doorway. When she left her father's ranch, Ida felt sorry that Willie couldn't come along. But now she was glad he had stayed home. "I rejoiced now that he too was not a victim," Ida said. "I thought how fortunate that he would be left for father and mother."[11] She also thought about her twenty-eight-year-old brother, George, and how distressed he would be when he heard his siblings were dead.

"I did not know what had become of the balance of the party, but supposed that they were all dead, and expected that Emma and I were to be killed soon."[12]

While Ida rode on, the trail grew dark in the thick pine forest and the wind began to blow. She said she had never heard the wind make such a sad and mournful sound. The Indians' yells and whoops as they drove their horses echoed across the mountains, chilling her heart. She wished the Indians would kill her and be done with it. "I trembled with fear," she said. "I had read of savages burning their captives alive, and I thought that was why they were carrying us. I wished they would kill us instantly, and thus relieve us of our suffering."[13]

Ida had to cling tightly to the man ahead of her on the horse to keep from falling when the trail grew steep at the summit. Things got easier after they crossed the divide where the forest was broken with meadows and glades. As the sun began setting, Ida and her companion reached a valley where Indian women were building fires. The Indians took Ida to the middle of the camp where the women gave her a supper of bread and willow bark tea.

"The tea was so bitter," Ida said. "I could not drink it. I could not eat, although they insisted on my doing so. They were very kind to me."[14]

Ida spent the night sleeping on a buffalo robe surrounded by Indian women. In the morning, she began to look for Emma. After a while, she saw her big sister on a horse led by Poker Joe.

Ida exclaimed, "Oh, how I rejoiced to see her."[15] Emma reported that Frank was alive, and soon the Indians took the sisters to him.

While Ida and Emma talked, Poker Joe circled the camp issuing marching orders and getting the Indians ready to move. Then he and Frank joined Emma and Ida, and the four of them rode together. About noon, the Indians reached the Yellowstone River and began crossing. After watching the Indians for a while, Emma and her companions plunged into the river and swam their horses to the other side.

After the crossing, the Indians set up a camp on the east side of the Yellowstone River. They didn't know that members of the Helena Party, a group of ten men who had entered the park from the north via Mammoth Hot Springs, had seen their camp. The Helena Party beat a hasty retreat and camped in a secluded spot that they thought was safe from Indian attack.

After the Nez Perce finished crossing the Yellowstone River, the Indian women prepared a noon meal. Emma forced down some bread but didn't eat anything else. The women offered her fish, but she declined because she had seen how they were cooked. She described the fish preparation this way: "From a great string of fish the largest were selected, cut in two, dumped into a camp kettle filled with water, and boiled to a pulp." She added, "The formality of cleaning had not entered into the formula. While I admit that tastes differ, I prefer having them dressed."[16]

* * * *

Later that afternoon, Emma and her siblings sat in the shade of a tree and watched the Indians hold a council to decide what to do with them. Seven chiefs sat in a circle and passed a long-stemmed pipe to each other. In turn, each took a few puffs, then rose to speak. Poker Joe interpreted the proceedings for the audience.

After a while, Poker Joe said the council had decided to let Emma and Ida go with the man they had captured the afternoon before, but they wanted to hold Frank and Shively for guides. The captured man was James Irwin, who had recently been discharged from the army at Fort Ellis. Irwin was still wearing army trousers, so Emma thought he was a deserter and didn't trust him. She refused to go with Irwin and demanded the Indians release Frank. The council resumed and finally acceded to Emma's demand that they release her and Ida with Frank.

The Indians provided the siblings with some bedding, a waterproof tarp, a jacket for Ida, bread, matches, and two worn-out horses for the women. Apparently, the Indians wanted Frank to walk so the trio would travel slowly. That would keep them from getting information about their captors' location to the army quickly.

The trio sadly clasped hands with Shively and promised to deliver messages to his friends if they escaped successfully. Emma said Shively's "eyes were dim with tears,"[17] but she considered his chances of escape better than her own because the Indians needed him to guide them.

Emma worried that she and her siblings would be attacked by scouts who were patrolling the area around the main Nez Perce camp. "We may be intercepted by warriors out of camp,"[18] she said.

Shively didn't think so. "No," he replied. "Something tells me you will get out safely."[19]

After they said goodbye to Shively, Emma and Ida mounted their horses, and Poker Joe rode up and ordered Frank to ride behind him. Then the group plunged into the Yellowstone River and swam across.

On the west side of the river, Poker Joe pointed to a clear trail that ran along the river and told the trio that they had to follow it: "All night. All Day. No sleep."[20] He said they could reach Bozeman in three days and repeated again that they had to travel night and day.

Joe shook hands with Frank, Emma, and Ida and said goodbye, and the siblings departed. The trio had gone only two hundred yards when they heard a horse galloping after them. Poker Joe approached and addressed the travelers. Frank reported his admonition like this: "Me want you to tell'm people in Bozeman me no fight no more. Me no want fight Montana Citizens.... Me want peace. You tell'm Bozeman people."[21]

Poker Joe became agitated and continued his plea for peace for a long time. Emma later recalled, "I thought he would never stop talking."[22]

Frank promised to spread the message and thanked Poker Joe for setting him and his sisters free. Frank also promised to help Poker Joe if the army ever caught him. Frank reported his promise in pidgin: "Maybe sometime soldiers catch'm you, me save you maybe. Me try anyway."[23]

"My friend," Poker Joe replied, "soldiers never take me alive, me die first."[24] He did "die first"—defending his people at the Battle of Bear Paw a few weeks later when the army finally defeated the Nez Perce and took most of them captive.

Goodbyes were exchanged again, and the siblings headed northward down the Yellowstone River with the sisters on horses and Frank walking. The Indians had set them free—free in the middle of a roadless wilderness where young warriors were stealing horses and killing white people.

They traveled slowly because of the worn-out horses, and because they could go no faster than Frank could walk. After a few miles they disregarded Poker Joe's admonition to stay on the trail and veered off into the timber so they could keep out of sight. After a few miles they came to the Hayden Valley with its wide expanses of meadow. They decided to hide on a timbered knoll for nightfall so they could cross in darkness. The moon was just past full that night of August 25, and it must have made the valley glow. The siblings waited until 2 a.m. when the moon had gone down to start across the valley so Indians couldn't see them.

One of the valley's huge washouts obstructed their way, and they had to search for hours for a place where they could cross. The sun was already up before they reached the timber at the head of the trail to the Yellowstone Falls. As they moved along the trail, they kept a sharp eye out for hostile Indians and for soldiers they hoped were in the area.

Near the falls, they heard the sound of wood chopping but decided to rush on rather than investigate. Frank said later that the sound must have come from the Helena Party's camp, which couldn't have been more than a half-mile away. "If I had known it," he said, "I could have warned them,"[25] and lives would have been saved.

The siblings tried to hurry, but their tired horses could barely match Frank's walking speed. They passed the point where the Indians had brought them across the Mary Mountain trail the day before. Emma wanted to return that way to look for her husband, George Cowan, but Frank talked her out of that. Frank said Poker Joe warned him that Nez Perce warriors had gone that way to intercept the pursuing army.

Emma said, "We dared not retrace that route, even though my husband's body lay dead there—dead and unburied, perhaps dragged and torn by wild beasts."[26] It was August 26, just one day after Emma and George's second wedding anniversary.

The siblings passed close enough to the Lower Falls of the Yellowstone to hear them roaring, but then they rushed onward. They found horse tracks in the trail that Frank thought must have been left by Texas Jack Omohundro and the men he was guiding. The tracks looked fresh, and the siblings hoped to catch up to the showman and get help.

By 8 a.m. they were at the base of Mount Washburn, and they made it to the summit by 3 that afternoon. It was frigid at the mountain top, and the travelers were exhausted. They headed down the mountain, turning back and forth along the switchbacks of the rocky trail. Occasionally, they could see the tracks of Texas Jack's party and that prompted them to hurry.

After an hour or so they regained sight of the Yellowstone River. Frank said he looked back toward Mount Washburn and saw "falls coming from the snow and falling hundreds of feet. They looked like bands of silver," he said.[27]

When he pointed the falls out to Emma, she said she recognized it as Tower Fall, which she had seen four years before when she visited the Mammoth Hot Springs with her parents. "We cannot be far from the Springs now," Emma said. "Let us hurry on and we will find help there."[28]

They began the descent down the canyon in front of Tower Fall and were at Tower Creek by late afternoon. There they found the spot where the Helena Party had camped two days before on the first night after they left Mammoth Hot Springs. The siblings searched the campsite and found scraps of dried-out bread—their first food of the day.

After they finished their morsels, they rested in the shade of a large pine. Frank looked up and spotted a note that the Helena Party had left on the morning of August 24. He took down the note, added a statement on the

The Lower Falls of the Yellowstone River was a major landmark for tourists traveling through Yellowstone Park in the 1870s.

NATIONAL PARK SERVICE PHOTO BY WILLIAM HENRY JACKSON, 1871

back with his own name and the names of his sisters, and said they were all that was left of a party of ten. He put the note back in the tree.

The siblings resumed their journey, crossing the creek and climbing the mountain on the other side. The path was so steep that the sisters had to dismount and walk. The women clutched the tails of their horses to help them climb the steep slope, and Frank followed them. When they reached the top, Frank helped them mount and resumed the lead.

Frank's head poked through the crown of his ruined hat, and the tattered brim flapped up and down on his neck as he walked. Still, it protected his neck from the sun that blazed through the thin mountain air. Ida and Emma, sunburned in their torn, dirty dresses, followed him. They had traveled about fifteen miles when Frank spotted several horses grazing on the mountainside.

"Look out," he said, and the women jumped off their horses and scurried into the timber to hide. Frank dropped to his knees and crawled to the crest of the hill where he could see a curl of smoke rising above a clump of bushes beyond a small stream. There were people behind those bushes, but Frank needed to know what kind of people. Were they carefree tourists like he and his sisters had been just a few days ago, or hostile Indians like those who had attacked them, or—best of all—soldiers on patrol? Frank knew he had to protect the women. He had to be sure they were safe. He waited and watched.

He waited even after he saw a soldier in a blue cavalry uniform. That soldier might be a captive like James Irwin, the man back at the Nez Perce camp, he thought. Another soldier stood, then another. Salvation was at hand.

He ran back to his sisters and announced, "We are safe. They are soldiers."[29] Then he dashed away leaving them to follow. He strode into the cavalry camp and greeted the officer in charge, "How are you, Lieutenant?"[30]

The startled young officer was Lieutenant Robert Schofield, who was leading a scouting party from Fort Ellis, the military post near Bozeman. He was one of the dozens of soldiers and civilian scouts who were looking for the Nez Perce. The memory of the Battle of the Little Bighorn where a coalition of Sioux and Cheyenne wiped out Colonel George Armstrong Custer and his men must have haunted the scouts as they searched. Telegraph lines had spread the news that the Nez Perce had almost given Colonel John Gibbon and his men the same fate in a fierce battle near the Big Hole River two weeks earlier.

Tower Fall was a camping point for Yellowstone Park travelers. Emma
Cowan and her siblings found food scraps there after the Nez Perce
released them.

NATIONAL PARK SERVICE PHOTO BY WILLIAM HENRY JACKSON, 1871

By the time Lieutenant Schofield encountered the tourists, he had already scanned the area from the top of Mount Washburn and concluded there were no Indians around. He planned to head back to Fort Ellis the next morning to report that.

In response to Frank's greeting, Lieutenant Schofield replied, "How are you, sir?"[31] He looked the disheveled man up and down.

Frank ignored the query. "Got anything to eat?"[32] he asked.

"Yes," the lieutenant replied, and then he looked up the hill.

"Who are those young ladies coming down the hill?"[33] he asked.

Frank explained that the elder woman was his twenty-three-year-old sister, Emma Cowan, whose husband had been shot by the Indians. The younger one was their thirteen-year-old sister, Ida Carpenter.

"We are all that is left of a party of ten,"[34] Frank told the lieutenant. Frank said while the Indians were shooting Emma's husband, George, in the head, his friends made a break for the trees. But he heard gunshots in the forest and he assumed—erroneously, it turned out—that all of them had been killed. In fact, they all had survived.

The soldiers gave the women soap so they could clean themselves up and prepared a hearty meal for the famished refugees. Then Lieutenant Schofield saw a bedraggled man coming down the hill.

Frank jumped up and looked at the approaching man. "That's none of our party," he said. "I guess it's one of the Helena Boys."[35]

When the man arrived, Frank asked, "Are you one of the Helena Party?"[36]

"Yes, my name is Pfister,"[37] the young man replied.

After the excitement caused by Fred Pfister's arrival had subsided, Lieutenant Schofield asked about his friends. Pfister said when the Helena Party saw Indians the day before near Sulphur Mountain, they withdrew about four miles and camped in a secluded spot where they thought they wouldn't be found.

In the morning, two men went scouting to see if it was safe to travel. The Indians attacked the camp about noon.

"I don't think any of the boys got away," Pfister said. That was another exaggeration of the number dead. In fact, the Indians had killed only one man when they attacked the Helena Party. The other men had escaped into the wilderness and were struggling toward safety. Army couriers carried reports like Pfister's back to Montana towns where newspapers printed sensational stories under headlines like "The National Park Massacres: Fifteen of the Helena and Radersburg Excursionists Supposed to Have Been Murdered."[38]

Although the soldiers had prepared to spend the night, Lieutenant Schofield decided to break camp and take the bedraggled refugees to the relative comfort and safety of Mammoth Hot Springs, which was only about twelve miles away.

The sun soon set, and they traveled along before the moon rose. It was a dark, cloudy night, so the soldiers had to lead their horses over the rocky trail through the Gardner River Canyon. They could hear the rapids roaring hundreds of feet below but couldn't see the river.

When they finally arrived at McCartney's cabin at Mammoth Hot Springs, they found its owner, James McCartney, and another group of tourists who had fled the Nez Perce: Texas Jack Omohundro and the two Englishmen he had been guiding through the park. Emma wrote, "One of these gentlemen was a physician and kindly assisted in dressing the wounds. I am sure he never found a time when his services were more appreciated."[39]

About 11 p.m. Lieutenant Schofield came to McCartney's cabin and announced he was sending a courier to Fort Ellis. He offered to include messages from the tourists in the courier's packet. Frank drafted a note to be sent by telegram to his brother, George, in Helena: "Emma, Ida and myself are alive; Cowan and Al Oldham are killed. I saw Cowan and Oldham shot. The balance are missing. I think all are killed: don't know but will send particulars when I reach Bozeman. Helena party all gone except one; all are missing. Indians fired into their camp."

Fred Pfister also sent a message: "Our party were attack today about noon. I am the only one so far as known that escaped them. Probably they will come in tonight. I will give particulars from Bozeman."

Mounted couriers rushed the two messages, along with the report Lieutenant Schofield dispatched to his superiors, to the telegraph office in Fort Ellis the night of August 26. They were printed in an extra edition of the *Helena Herald* on August 27. The news of massacres in Yellowstone Park spread to newspapers across Montana Territory and the nation by telegraph.

Before dawn on August 26, everybody in the cabin was awakened by the sound of horses and someone calling, "Roll out and let us in."[40] It was four more members of the Helena Party. Two of the men were wounded. Andrew Weikert had a flesh wound in his shoulder, and Jack Stewart had more serious injuries: gunshots in his thigh and ankle. The other arrivals were Leslie Wilkie and Ben Stone. That left eleven tourists still unaccounted for: five from the Helena Party and six from the Radersburg Party.

The next morning Fred Pfister left for Fort Ellis with Lieutenant Schofield and his men. Later, the pioneer Yellowstone Park photographer Henry "Bird" Calfee arrived at McCartney's. Calfee offered to take the tourists to Bozeman in the large wagon he used to haul his bulky photographic equipment. Emma and Ida rode in the wagon. It's not clear if the two Englishmen were in the wagon or riding horses. Texas Jack and Frank Carpenter rode along behind the wagon and watched for Indians.

After a few miles, Texas Jack pointed his spyglass up the Gardner Canyon toward the route the tourists had traversed with Lieutenant Schofield the night before. The showman told Frank he saw five or six Indians chasing two white men. Frank said he later learned that the two men were Leander Duncan and Richard Dietrich of the Helena Party, but those men never reported seeing Indians on their way back to McCartney's. Texas Jack told Frank to stay with the wagon and said, "I'll go back and give those Indians a shot or two."[41]

Frank said the wagon rushed away and was about three miles ahead when he heard several gunshots ring out to the rear. Texas Jack rejoined them, and he said he had shot two Indian ponies and driven the Indians away. "The news relieved our anxiety considerably," Frank said, "and we began to breathe easier."[42]

Emma dismissed Texas Jack's story as "a somewhat amusing incident."[43] She said no one else saw the Indians Texas Jack reported before he dashed away. When the guide returned, he declared the Indians had shot at him and offered a bullet hole through the bottom of his stirrup as evidence.

Emma said the Englishmen that Jack was guiding were skeptical. "They examined the stirrup and asked him why the splinters all pointed down. It was apparent that the hole could have been made only by removing his foot and firing the shot himself."[44]

Apparently, Texas Jack was trying to build his reputation as an Indian fighter so he could promote the Wild West stage show he starred in and took across the country immediately after he left the park. In October, he was telling newspaper reporters that he had escorted Emma Cowan and Ida and Frank Carpenter to safety in Bozeman.

"I protected the rear," Texas Jack told a New York newspaper, "and several times we were fired upon by Nez Perces Indians. I had my stirrup shot away and a ball shot through my hand."[45] Neither Emma nor Frank recalled multiple Nez Perce attacks or Texas Jack being shot.[46]

After Texas Jack rejoined the group, they traveled on and reached Bottlers Ranch forty miles north of Mammoth Hot Springs that evening. Emma said that everybody at Bottlers was "rife with excitement," and people all over Montana feared raids by the Nez Perce. At the same time, Emma added, Crow Indians, whose reservation was just across the Yellowstone River from Bottlers, "took advantage of the fact, and numerous horse-stealing raids occurred for which the Nez Perce received the credit."[47]

Also at Bottlers, Texas Jack gave Ida Carpenter a pair of beaded moccasins that Frank described as "very acceptable," but Emma dismissed as a "bogus 50-cent pair."[48]

The next day the photographer, Henry "Bird" Calfee, decided to record the event with his camera. He took a photo of Emma Cowan and her siblings, Frank and Ida Carpenter, along with Texas Jack Omohundro and the men who went through the park with him.

Friends of Emma's in Bozeman had heard of her plight, apparently from army couriers, and sent a carriage to retrieve her and Ida. The carriage arrived in the morning, so they were on their way to Bozeman by noon. They made twelve miles of the forty-mile trip and stopped at a ranch on Trail Creek Pass. That evening, Emma recounted her adventure with the Nez Perce, and the ranchers' children listened with rapt attention. Living close to the Crow Reservation, the children were used to Indian scares and told Emma what they would do if they were captured. They said they would escape and live on camas root.

That evening after everyone had gone to bed, a neighbor tapped at the ranch house door and quietly told everybody to get dressed because there were Indians around. Emma said that caused "a scrambling for clothes in the dark," and "a regular mix-up of children and clothes occurred, which a mother alone could straighten out."

While the women hid in the ranch house, the men grabbed their guns and went out to confront the Indians. Several shots were fired, and the Indians disappeared. Emma said, "We retired again, but did not sleep much."[49]

The next day, the tourists returned to Bozeman. On the way they met Lieutenant Gustavus Doane accompanied by a contingent of soldiers from Fort Ellis and about eighty Crow Indians he had recruited to fight the Nez Perce.[50] Doane was on his way to Yellowstone Park to contain the Nez Perce there.

After Frank escorted his sisters to Bozeman the next day, he borrowed a horse and joined a group of men headed to the park to find and bury the bodies of George and the other presumed dead. Emma and Ida rested at Bozeman's finest hotel, the Northern Pacific, which was named in anticipation of the railroad's arrival. After a few days, they returned to their parents' ranch near Radersburg.

While Emma waited, reports kept dribbling back from Yellowstone Park that General O. O. Howard's scouts had found survivors of Nez Perce attacks. Those reports with headlines like "The Escape of Roberts, Foller, Wilke, Stuart, and Others of the Party," and "The Escape of William Dingee and A. J. Arnold"[51] sustained Emma's hope that George would be found alive.

CHAPTER 11
Ben Stone Escapes

On the morning of August 26, members of the Helena Party hung around their camp trading jokes with their African American cook, Ben Stone. Although they had rushed into hiding the day before when they saw six hundred Indians crossing the Yellowstone River, they felt safe. Their hiding place was a mile and a half off the beaten path. It sat on a triangular knoll between the forks of Otter Creek and was out of sight behind the crest of the hill. A lookout on the top of the hill could have monitored approaches from all directions, but the tourists didn't think they needed to post a guard.[1]

Two of the party's most able outdoorsmen, Andy Weikert and Leslie Wilkie, had gone out to make sure the Indians moved on and were no longer a threat. The scouts said they would fire rifle shots as a warning if they saw hostiles, but that seemed unlikely.

Still, some of the men were worried. Charles Kenck, the party's only married man, had left by himself the day before and raced toward home, but he rejoined the group when nobody followed him. Jack Stewart told Kenck that if he didn't feel safe he could pick any two horses he wanted and go home via Mammoth Hot Springs, but Kenck said he would stay with the group.

Stone tried to cheer the men with joking banter. Leander Duncan was particularly downhearted, so Stone told him that at his age he "should be thinking of his girl instead of Indians."[2]

Young Joe Roberts spoke up. "Ben, you're gassing too much. What would you do if the Indians do come after us?"[3]

Stone told Roberts to take care of himself and resumed his amusing banter. The group's laughter was interrupted by Kenck, who had been asleep and wanted to know what was so funny.

"Now tell me, Ben," Kenck demanded, "so I can laugh too."[4] Stone was just starting to reply when rifle shots rang out.

When Stone heard the first shots, he thought Weikert and Wilkie were just trying to scare everybody. He called out for the men to stop their foolishness because somebody might get hurt. But when the second volley came, he looked around and saw his companions running for cover and joined them. Stone tumbled down the hill, turning three somersaults to the bottom near a creek. He looked up and saw an Indian about twenty yards away. "I'm a goner,"[5] he said.

A bullet hit the ground near Stone, so he rolled into the creek. As he lay in the frigid water, he heard Indians plundering the camp. Stone started shivering so hard that he muddied the creek. He knew he had to stop shuddering because there were Indians below who might see the muddy water.

He tried to climb out of the creek but tumbled back in when he heard two rifle shots a hundred yards away. He stayed in the creek until everything was quiet—nearly three hours.

When Stone finally got out of the creek he saw his hat had washed downstream about fifteen yards. When he went to retrieve it, he stumbled from exhaustion. But he got up again and made his way up the stream, across a marsh and into the timber. He hiked to the main trail and started toward Yellowstone Falls. He soon came to the spot where his party had camped two days before. He searched the area and found two bacon rinds, declared them "pretty good grub,"[6] ate one, and pocketed the other.

Glancing into a tree, Stone saw a small piece of paper. He took it down and read the note: "I have been waiting for you. Am now going to the springs. Will wait for you there. —C.M.K."[7]

Stone knew the note was from Charles Kenck and decided to get to Mammoth Hot Springs as soon as he could. He figured it was about thirty-five miles and he could make it by sunup the next day. Stone's hope of seeing Kenck again was in vain. Indians had shot Kenck to death hours earlier. The note was from the day before when Kenck had made his aborted attempt to rush home and then returned to the main party. If he had continued to Mammoth Hot Springs, Kenck probably would have saved his life and been able to rejoin his wife and infant daughter in Helena.

Later that day while crossing a prairie, Stone looked back and saw a dark object following him. He hid in the timber behind a marshy spot and waited for an hour and a half. As the object drew nearer, Stone could see that it was someone on horseback, but he couldn't tell if it was a white man or an Indian.

Jack Stewart finally arrived and called out, "My God, Ben! Is that you?"[8] Stone said he thought it was.

Stewart asked about the rest of the party, and Stone told him about Kenck's note.

"Thank God for that,"[9] Stewart replied.

Stone said, "Let's travel lively and get out of here."[10] But then he saw blood running down the side of Stewart's horse. He helped the injured man down and tended his wounds. Then the pair sat on a log to eat lunch from the food Stewart had packed in his coat pockets. They shared their stories of what had just happened to them.

Stewart said he was trying to catch up on his sleep when the Indians attacked. He jumped up and ran. One bullet hit his leg and another his hip. As he fell he heard Charles Kenck yell out, "I am murdered."[11]

While one Indian plundered Kenck's body, another approached Stewart. Seeing a gun pointed at his face, Stewart threw up his hands and begged for his life. The Indian set his rifle on its butt and asked Stewart if he had any money.

"I have a little,"[12] Stewart replied. The Indian shoved his hand into Stewart's left pocket, but there was nothing there. Then he rolled Stewart over and rifled his right pocket where he found $263 and a silver watch. The man who had plundered Kenck arrived, and the two Indians opened the money roll and laughed at their good fortune. They examined Stewart's bleeding wounds, told him they wouldn't kill him, and walked away.

Stewart lay still and watched the Indians search the camp for loot. He stayed in the grass for three hours. Then he tried to climb the hill to see if Kenck was still alive, but he couldn't do it. He called for help as loud as he could, but no one answered.

At last he slid down the hill on his hands and knees. When he reached the creek, he washed his wounds, drank several times, and rested. When he felt stronger, he made his way back to the camp, walking part of the way and crawling the rest.

He was surprised to find that when the Indians plundered the camp they left a lot of food behind. He sat and ate some bread and ham, which he said "refreshed me considerably."[13]

Stewart found his overcoat, stuffed the pockets with matches and food, and started to walk down the trail hoping to find help. After hobbling along for half a mile, he was startled by a neighing horse. He looked up the hill and saw his mare, Nellie. He called her by name and she came to him.

He caught Nellie's picket rope, which she had pulled loose when the Indians attacked. He led her up the hill to a big rock, crawled up on it, and tried to get on Nellie's back. But he couldn't keep his balance and slid off the other side. The pain of the fall stunned him, and he lay on the ground for fifteen minutes. Then he crawled to the rock and tried again. Again he lost his balance and fell off the other side of the horse.

Nellie seemed puzzled and stood perfectly still. She stuck her nose under Stewart's coat and sniffed the blood there. Stewart said she "acted just as if she wanted to express her sympathy in words, but didn't have them at her command."[14]

Stewart quit trying to ride and began hobbling down the trail. Nellie followed. Stewart picked up a stout stick and used it to support the weight on his right side when he climbed uphill. Going downhill, he sat and used his left leg to pull himself along.

When he got to Cascade Creek near the falls of the Yellowstone, Stewart washed his wounds, ate, drank, and started again. About half a mile north of the falls, Nellie followed Stewart into a little ravine where he climbed the bank and managed to mount her. They traveled just another mile when Stewart spotted Ben Stone waiting in some fallen timber.

After Stewart and Stone finished trading stories, they started on toward Mammoth Hot Springs. Stewart said he couldn't ride anymore and hobbled along bracing his wounded leg with a stick.

Stewart and Stone had gone just ten feet when they heard the tramp of horses behind them. Stewart turned and exclaimed, "Thank God! Here comes Wilkie and Weikert."[15]

Leslie Wilkie and Andy Weikert caught up with them. Stewart explained that his injuries kept him from riding up and down hills without a saddle, so Wilkie lent him his horse. Stone mounted Weikert's horse, and Weikert and Wilkie took turns riding Stewart's Nellie. The group arrived at Mammoth Hot Springs early the next morning where they found McCartney's cabin filled with tourists fleeing the Nez Perce.

One of the men at McCartney's was an English physician who was touring the park with the showman Texas Jack Omohundro. The doctor treated Stewart's wounded leg and hip and the gash in Weikert's shoulder.

Wilkie immediately rode away with the army scouts who had rescued Emma Cowan, her siblings, and Fred Pfister. He went to summon an ambulance to take Stewart to Bozeman for medical help. The soldiers were returning to Fort Ellis, and Bozeman was just a few miles west of there.

Most of the other tourists at McCartney's departed the next day in a freight wagon. But Weikert decided to stay at McCartney's and see if any other members of the Helena Party would show up. He waited two days, but when Charles Kenck, Joe Roberts, and August Foller didn't arrive, Weikert decided to return to the wilderness to search for them. He planned to leave that afternoon and travel through the night, but the owner of the cabin, Jim McCartney, talked him out of it. McCartney agreed to go with Weikert if they could leave the next morning.

After Weikert and McCartney moved into the wilderness to find Joe Roberts, August Foller, and Charles Kenck, an ambulance arrived to haul Jack Stewart back to Bozeman. The ambulance men begged Richard Dietrich to go with them, but the music professor said he had to wait and see if Weikert and McCartney could find Joe Roberts.

When Dietrich insisted on remaining at Mammoth Hot Springs, the cook, Ben Stone, decided to stay too. If any of the party came in, Stone wanted to be available to feed them and nurse their wounds. One of the ambulance men, Jake Stoner, decided to stay with Dietrich and Stone.

After the ambulance left, Dietrich and Stoner went fishing. They returned about 3 p.m., and Stone fixed them a meal. Then Stone and Dietrich decided to take a bath in the hot pools. Stoner said he would go with them to see the Mammoth Hot Springs and took his gun "to knock over a grouse" because "grub was getting scarce."[16]

When they finished bathing, Dietrich and Stone returned to the cabin. Then Dietrich went out again to water the horses and move their pickets so the animals could graze on fresh pasture.

Stone sat down in the cabin door and glanced toward the springs. He saw the teamster Stoner running toward him and asked if he had caught a grouse.

"No," Stoner replied, "I've caught something else."[17] Then Stoner explained that while he was standing on the mountain at the top of the springs, he saw a group of mounted men heading slowly toward him.

"You did!" Stone replied. "Andy and McCartney have found the boys and are bringing them in. Of course, they are wounded and have to travel slowly. I'll go in the house, make a fire, and have grub ready for the boys by the time they get here."[18]

"No," the teamster countered, "don't do that. We had better cache our-selves in the timber until we know if they're white men or not."[19]

"Good idea," Stone replied.

Then the teamster asked where Dietrich was, saying, "I'll warn him so he can take to the timber too."[20]

Stone replied that the music professor was on the flat tending the horses, so Stoner rushed off. Then Stone started up the gulch behind the cabin to hide. After going about twenty-five yards, he turned into the timber and climbed a point of rocks that overlooked the area. From there he could see all the trails that led to the cabin.

He stood there about twenty minutes but saw nothing. Then he sat down to wait. Still nothing came into view. Risking being seen, he went forward to a better vantage point.

Then he saw something in the distance, a man wearing a white blanket. The blanketed man dodged out of sight like he was trying to hide. Then another man in a blanket appeared. Then another.

Stone knew he was seeing Indians and decided to head deeper into the timber. He saw Indians ahead of him and ran. He stepped on a dead branch, and it broke with a loud crash. The Indians heard the crash and rushed toward it. Stone knew that if he didn't hide he would be a dead man.

He heard twigs breaking ahead of him, so he knew an Indian was close. Just when he thought he was doomed, he ran under the low branches of a tree. He grabbed a branch and hoisted himself up. As soon as he got into the tree, a mounted Indian rode under it, looking in every direction to see what had made the noise—every direction but straight up. Stone hugged the tree and held his breath. He later said the Indian was so close that he could have stepped on the man's head.

The Indian rode on about ten yards, raised his gun on his arm, and stopped to listen. Hearing nothing, he rode away.

Stone figured he was safe hidden in the tree, so he stayed there for two more hours. While he waited, he heard gunshots coming from the direction of the cabin. After dark, Stone left his perch and headed up a mountain. He crawled because he feared that if he walked he would knock rocks loose and the clatter would attract Indians. When he reached the mountaintop, he lay down and rested. He decided to head down the valley to Henderson's Ranch, which was a few miles distant just outside the park boundary.

Fearing Indians might still be around, he stayed deep in the timber as he moved along. Then he was startled by a great crash. When he looked up, Stone saw a bear in the bright moonlight. He said the bear looked at him and gave a bear laugh. Stone decided he preferred bears to Indians and waited. The bear gave another laugh and then left. Stone thought the devil himself couldn't find him in thick timber and waited there through the night and all the next day.

About 3 p.m., he heard shots coming from the direction of the cabin and figured the Indians had found Stoner and Dietrich. Two hours later, he heard two more shots that he thought must be Stoner defending himself. "Good boy, Jake," he thought, "stand 'em off."[21]

As darkness fell, Stone left the thick timber about three miles below Mammoth Hot Springs. As he headed down the trail, he heard another gunshot from the direction of the cabin. He was glad to be away from the fighting.

Stone kept moving hoping to find help before daylight. Whenever he heard any noise ahead, he hid until he was sure there weren't any Indians coming.

After three hours he figured he must be getting close to Henderson's Ranch. Then he heard a tinkling cowbell. Peering ahead, he saw some sort of camp silhouetted by a nearby stream. It might be an Indian camp, he thought. He tried to see which it had, teepees or tents, but he couldn't tell. Finally, he decided to take his chances and go on.

He had gone only a few steps when he heard a voice call out, "Who goes there?"[22]

"A friend," Stone replied.

"What name?"

"Ben Stone."

"Come quick."

When Stone advanced, a soldier took his hand. The soldier took Stone to his lieutenant and said, "Here is the colored man we were looking for today."[23]

The lieutenant told Stone that his men had found Richard Dietrich dead in the cabin doorway at Mammoth. Dietrich had been shot three times, once through the heart.

Stone told the lieutenant there was another man, Jake Stoner, at Mammoth. Stoner had to still be alive, Stone said, because he heard gunshots near the cabin that afternoon. The lieutenant said someone else must have fired the shots because it was Stoner who told the soldiers to search for Ben Stone and Richard Dietrich.

Later that night, Andy Weikert and Jim McCartney arrived at the army camp. They had buried Kenck, but could not find Joe Roberts and August Foller. After Stone got to Bozeman, he learned that Joe and August had been rescued by teamsters with General Howard's army and made their way to Virginia City. Ben Stone went back to Helena and resumed his work as a cook.

CHAPTER 12

George's Ordeal

When George Cowan came to, he could tell it was late afternoon because the sun had started sliding behind the tops of the tall trees. He felt buzzing and dizziness in his numb head. The sensation grew lighter and lighter, and his head felt as large as a mountain. He raised his hand slowly and felt blood covering his face and lying clotted in his hair. He wiped the blood from his eyes and pulled off his hat. It was covered with skin and blood clots.

George ran his hand over his head and felt gashes in his scalp. He remembered the Indian pointing the navy revolver at his head and pulling the trigger. He thought the bullet must have passed through his head. Later an army surgeon would dig the slug out of his forehead and give it to George for a souvenir. He wore it as a watch fob for the rest of his life. Apparently, the pistol used to shoot George was loaded with a faulty charge so the bullet failed to penetrate his skull.

George examined his numb leg at the location of another bullet wound, but he couldn't find any broken bones. He felt an intolerable thirst, so he rose up on his elbow to look. He was about ten feet from the spot where he had been shot. Apparently, he got the gashes on his head when the Indians dragged him away by his feet.

The only sound he could hear was a light wind moaning in the trees, so he figured the Indians were gone. He reached for the bough of a small pine tree and pulled himself to his feet. As he rose, he saw an Indian watching him from the back of a pony.

As George hobbled away, he glanced over his shoulder and saw the Indian kneeling on one knee and taking aim. Then he heard the gun blast and felt a twinge in his left side. He dropped forward on his face. The bullet had hit him above his hip and come out in front of his abdomen.

George lay motionless, expecting that at any moment the Indian would dispatch him with a single swing of a hatchet. George said, "I must have lain

George Cowan was shot and left for dead on August 24, 1877. Unable to walk, he crawled for days seeking help. After the army found him, they hauled him across the roadless wilderness in a wagon for a grueling ride.

MONTANA HISTORICAL SOCIETY PHOTO

here fully 20 minutes expecting to die every moment, and during the time I think my mind must have dwelt on every incident of our trip."[1]

While George waited for a deadly hatchet blow, he anguished over the possibility that his wife, Emma, and her thirteen-year-old sister had been taken captive. The popular press of the era was filled with lurid stories of Indians torturing, raping, and enslaving white women. George must have known of such tales.

He later recalled, "I supposed my wife had not been killed. I knew the fate to which she and Ida would be subjected, and my whole nature was aroused as I thought of it."[2]

George heard Indians talking as they came up the trail driving horses. They passed within forty feet of where he lay motionless, and then the sound of their voices disappeared. He waited a while, then rolled over and looked around. The Indians were gone.

The passing of time and loss of blood left George so thirsty that he had to have water. He tried to get up but discovered that both of his legs were paralyzed, so he rolled onto his belly. By dragging himself with his elbows, he managed to move, but the mode of travel exhausted him and forced him to stop frequently to rest.

When he came to a small, warm stream, he rose on his hands and entered the water. He sank to his shoulders in mud and water came up to his chin, so he drank deeply. Then he pulled himself across the stream and tore apart some of his underwear with his teeth to make crude bandages for his wounds.

He crawled downstream for half a mile. By two o'clock in the morning he was exhausted and lay down to rest. At dawn he started again and crawled until noon, when he stopped to rest. After a few moments, he heard Indians coming down the trail. He stayed still, and the Indians soon passed.

George rested for an hour and resumed his journey. By nightfall he had gone four or five miles. He continued crawling through the moonlit night.

His wounds hurt and still bled, but that didn't bother him as much as the intense cold. He had had nothing to eat and his clothing was soaked with blood, mud, and water, so he had to keep moving to stay warm.

George kept crawling along, keeping beside the trail so he could hide in the bushes whenever he heard Indians approaching. When the Nez Perce traveled, each lodge drove its horses separately from the others, so small groups passed down the trail for hours. With 125 lodges, it took about three hours for the main camp to pass. George had to scurry to the side of the road and hide over and over again.

By Monday he reached the spot where his party had abandoned their wagons. He saw some papers fastened to the trees and discovered they were Charles Mann's sketches of the trip. George also found pages from Frank Carpenter's journal skittered around. George crawled around to pick them up. "I supposed then that I would die here, and thought that the journal would tell them of the party and its capture."[3]

When George crawled up to the wagon, he discovered his faithful dog, Dido, cowering under it. She came bounding out and covered his face and wounds with caresses. George said, "The pleasure of the meeting was mutual."[4]

The Indians had torn apart two wheels of the surrey to use the lathe-turned hardwood spokes as handles for their riding whips. That left the box tipped onto the ground so George could search it without having to stand. He found some rags and men's underwear that he could use. But there was nothing to eat.

George remembered he had spilled some coffee at the party's last camp at the Lower Geyser Basin. He called Dido and began crawling with her walking at his side. The coffee was four miles away, but the starving man forced himself to ignore the distance and think only of food.

Suddenly, Dido stopped and growled. George said, "I grasped her by the neck, and placed my hand over her nose to keep her from making a noise. Peering through the brush, I saw two Indians sitting beneath a tree but a few feet from me."[5] George backed away and cautiously circled around them. He reached the campsite at the Lower Geyser Basin on Tuesday night.

As expected, he found a handful of coffee beans and some matches lying on the ground. He pounded the coffee into a fine powder, built a fire, and made coffee in an empty molasses can. George said, "I soon had some excellent hot coffee that refreshed me greatly. This was my first refreshment that I had taken in five days and nights."[6]

Caffeine and sugar from the residue in the molasses can stimulated George, and he began calculating his chances. He decided that things were looking a lot better. "I would not starve," he said. "I could, as a last resort, kill my dog and eat it."[7]

When he recalled his ordeal later, George said, "I shudder now, as I think of sacrificing my noble, faithful dog, one that money cannot purchase now, but circumstances were such that I did not view it then as I do now. The natural desire for life will force one to any necessity."[8]

George stayed at the Lower Geyser Basin through the night. With his strength regained from coffee and molasses, he began thinking about his ordeal. "I supposed that I was the only one of the party left," he later recalled, "unless it be my wife, and speculations upon her fate almost set me mad. It was horrible." George couldn't sleep. He said he "hailed with pleasure the break of day."[9] It was August 29—five days after the day George was shot.

He made more coffee, but the sustenance it gave only aggravated his horror. He decided to crawl farther in hopes of finding help and called Dido to join him. He was getting weaker and crawled only a little way before he had to stop and rest.

He crawled for a mile and a half and crossed the Firehole River, then made for a grove a quarter of a mile away. He came to some brush at the edge of the road about 2 o'clock but was too exhausted to go on. "It was an expiring effort," he said, "and having accomplished it, I gave myself up for dead."[10]

After lying in a stupor for two hours, he heard horses but was too exhausted to care anymore. When Dido began to growl, he didn't stop her.

The horses drew near, approached, and stopped. The riders had seen him. He looked up and saw that they were white.

"Who are you?" one of the men asked.

George told the scouts his name and asked if there was any news of Emma. When they told him there was none, he turned away. He said he would have been glad to have died.

While one of the men built a fire and made coffee, the other asked questions, but George didn't want to answer. The men said they were S. G. Fisher and J. W. Reddington, scouts from Howard's command.[11] They gave George some hardtack and a blanket and told him Howard's troops would arrive the next day. Then they went to find the scene of the massacre and bury bodies.

After George had eaten, his desire to live returned. "It seems the spirit of revenge took complete possession of me," George said. "I knew I would live and I took a solemn vow that I would devote the rest of my life to killing Indians, especially Nez Perce."[12]

George lay beside the road for another day. Then he heard cavalry. Soon General Howard and some of his officers rode up. A few minutes later, George's friend, A. J. Arnold, arrived and knelt beside him. The men grasped hands but didn't speak for several minutes.

Finally, George gasped, "My wife?"[13]

"No news yet, George,"[14] Arnold replied.

A. J. Arnold and William Dingee had straggled into General Howard's camp at Henrys Lake the day before. They discovered that William Harmon, the prospector who had joined the Radersburg Party at the Lower Geyser Basin, had gotten there ahead of them and told the soldiers the Indians had killed everybody. The army took this false news to the telegraph office in Virginia City, and it spread across Montana Territory. Dingee wanted to set the record straight, so he immediately caught a ride to Virginia City to report that at least three people had survived.

The soldiers gave Arnold some food, and after he finished eating a spare meal, General Howard summoned him to gather intelligence. Their conversation didn't go well.

"How far are the Indians ahead of us?"[15] General Howard asked.

"About seventy-five miles,"[16] Arnold said. Then he told the general he wanted to go back to the park to find out what happened to his friends.

"We do not want you to go back," Howard said. Then he tried to reassure Arnold, "We will look after your party and things."[17]

But Arnold insisted. "I am going back anyhow. I want to see what has become of the party. I have walked four days and nights without food, and can do it again if need be."[18]

When the general queried Arnold further, things got testy. Howard asked, "What were you doing in the basins—prospecting or trapping?"[19]

"We were there for pleasure," Arnold retorted.

The general started to lecture Arnold, "You ought to have known that the Indians were coming." But Arnold knew that Howard's commanding officer had just visited the park with a small escort. He snapped back, "So should General Sherman, then. Was he there prospecting or trapping?"[20] When the army headed into the park, Arnold went with them.

Two days after Arnold and Dingee arrived at Howard's camp, the army was at the headwaters of the Madison River, where teamsters brought in Al Oldham. Oldham had run into the timber when the Indians had accosted the Radersburg Party and they shot him. The bullet passed through both of his cheeks, leaving his head a bloody mess. When the Indians went to check the unconscious man, they saw blood oozing from his head, assumed the wound was fatal, and left him for dead. Later he regained consciousness and had been wandering alone in the wilderness for six days.

The day after the teamsters found Oldham, the army arrived at the Lower Geyser Basin and scouts brought George Cowan to the camp. George, who had been shot three times and couldn't walk, had been crawling through the wilderness for a week looking for help. Arnold described him this way: "George was a most pitiful object. He was covered with blood, which had dried on him, and he was as black as a Negro. His clothing was caked with dry mud, and his head looked like that of a tar-headed Indian in mourning for the dead."[21]

Arnold examined George's wounds and told him there were several surgeons with the army, so he should get medical attention soon. After that, General Howard and his staff mounted their horses and, saying they would camp nearby, left Arnold to tend George's wounds.

An ambulance finally arrived carrying Oldham, and George was put in it. An army surgeon told Arnold he would dress George's wounds when they arrived at camp. Arnold laid blankets under a tree and made a bed for George. They waited—but the surgeon didn't come. After a while, Arnold went in search for a doctor. He couldn't find one.

Later when George recalled his time with the army, he said of his treatment, "I cannot thank any of Howard's surgeons for my recovery, as Arnold could get no one to come to see me. One would send him to another, and he finally learned that they had all gone off with General Howard to see the geysers. The general and his staff were picnicking while settlers were being killed or dying all around them."[22]

At sundown, Arnold searched again and found a doctor named Fitzgerald. Dr. Fitzgerald said it was another doctor's job to look after George, but he would do it. Dr. Fitzgerald looked angry when he arrived. Arnold said the doctor probed for the bullet in George's head "in a manner not in keeping with the wounded man's condition."[23] After digging out the bullet, the surgeon announced it was not his job to dress the wounds and left. With help from enlisted men and teamsters, Arnold bandaged the wounds and dressed George with some clothes the enlisted men gave him.

The next morning a courier named Frank J. Parker came into camp from Bozeman. He saw George lying on the ground looking forlorn. The courier offered the suffering man consolation in the form of whiskey, but George turned it down and refused to talk.

"What's wrong with the fellow?"[24] the courier asked.

"If you were in his place you would feel the same way," one of the scouts replied. "That is Cowan."[25]

"What!" exclaimed the courier, "Why, I just came from Bozeman, and both his wife and her sister and their brother, Frank Carpenter, are there, unharmed."[26]

The courier went back to George and said, "Now you see here! I have the best news in the world for you, but I won't tell you a word until you take a good drink of this whiskey."[27]

George perked up and demanded the news, but the courier insisted that he take a drink. While George sipped the whiskey, the courier told him that Emma and her siblings were safe.

When he recalled the incident later, George said, "Before I was despondent, now everything wore a different aspect, and I could laugh and joke with all. The bright anticipations for the future, when my wife and I should be united, kept me up during the trials and sufferings of the days following, and probably did much to keep death at a distance."[28]

George wanted General Howard to send him home by way of the road to Henrys Lake, but Howard said he needed the best medical care and insisted that he stay with the army. Arnold said Howard promised to see to it that George got "the best of medical attendance," but he never delivered on that promise.

"The treatment that he received," Arnold said, "was to be placed in an old wagon and jolted over the worst road that ever was passed over by a wagon. The officers and surgeons would have let him rot alive. Some of the teamsters gave him underclothing, that was a great service to him, as his wounds discharged a great deal."[29]

Arnold said that if Indians had attacked the camp at the Lower Geyser Basin, "There would not have been an officer or a surgeon captured by the Indians. They were all off visiting the geysers."[30]

"I supposed Sherman was 'prospecting or trapping,'"[31] Arnold added sarcastically, referring to commanding General William Tecumseh Sherman's visit to the park a few days before.

Apparently unaware of his guests' dissatisfaction with their treatment, General Howard named the camp of August 30th "Camp Cowan" in honor of the injured lawyer.

The next day General Howard ordered his entourage of cavalry, infantry, road builders, and teamsters to follow the Indians up the creek the Nez Perce had traveled. The teamsters piled blankets in the bottom of a spring wagon to make a place for George and his dog to ride. The trail was choked with fallen timber and brush, so the ride was rough and progress was slow.

One of General Howard's teamsters, Henry Buck, reported that about halfway up the hill one of the teamsters exclaimed, "Oh, look there," and pointed over the rolling country to the south. Eight miles away the men saw a geyser spouting an enormous column of water and steam. It was the Excelsior Geyser, the largest in the world. During its greatest eruptions, the Excelsior hurled a column of water three hundred feet wide and three hundred feet high and made the ground shake like an earthquake. Most of its eruptions were less dramatic, and Buck's description is the only one of the 1877 eruption known. When the teamsters saw steam rising from the Lower Geyser Basin, curiosity overwhelmed them. They halted the wagons and climbed a hill to marvel at the panorama of boiling springs and geysers. After wandering over the white crust and inspecting the wonders for a while, they resumed their travels.

About a mile farther, the teamsters passed the spot at the end of the road where the Radersburg Party had abandoned their wagon and buggy and the Indians had ransacked them. "They were almost totally destroyed," Arnold said. "We gathered up what we could and carried the pieces with us."[32]

After the road ended, the teamsters continued up a trail that ran along the creek. Travel on the unimproved trail must have left poor George jostling and jolting as the wagon he was riding bounced over the rocks. At the base of Mary Mountain, the trail left the stream and headed up the mountainside through thick timber, a route that no wagon could follow.

General Howard decided to forge ahead with his soldiers, leaving the civilian teamsters and road builders behind to cut a new route through the timber and bring the wagons. That left the civilians without any protection. Arnold was disgusted. "We, who were left behind," he sarcastically remarked, "were well protected that night, as there was not a gun in the whole outfit."[33]

The men who stayed behind found an open meadow and camped for the night. The next morning forty horses that the teamsters had turned loose to graze were missing. The teamsters noticed Bannock Indian scouts who were supposed to be with Howard had lingered behind and dispatched a courier to General Howard's camp to ask for help. Howard sent an officer and detachment of cavalry to help recover the missing animals.

Howard said his men soon returned with ten Bannock scouts, and he ordered them to disarm the scouts and take their horses. An old chief who was the leader of the Indians protested and assured Howard the Indians hadn't taken the horses.

Howard said he told the chief, "What you say may be true, but Indians are good to hunt horses. They follow blind trails better than white men. Send out some of your young men and look up my lost horses. I will never set the prisoners free till the horses are brought back."[34]

Henry Buck, a teamster who traveled with Howard through the park, said the conversation was between the old chief and the officer Howard had sent to help the teamsters.[35] In any case, the old chief agreed that Indians were good at hunting horses and sent out a group of young men. A few hours later the young men galloped back to camp with about twenty horses. This didn't impress anybody, and the chief was told the captives wouldn't be released until the other horses were returned. The old chief grunted, shrugged his shoulders, and rode away. At dusk the remaining horses were returned and Howard released the prisoners, except for one who was apparently the ring leader of the would-be horse thieves.

The road builders laid out a route that zigzagged up the steep slope for three miles following ridges and gullies. Then they went to work cutting live trees and deadfall and rolling rocks out of the way. Two days later, a passable road was ready, but it went along steep side hills where the wagons might roll over. To keep the wagons from capsizing, the men fastened ropes to the top of the wagons and walked alongside them, holding firm. Poor George Cowan rode in one of these tipsy wagons with his dog, Dido, while it made its treacherous climb.

After they cleared the summit, the teamsters came to a slope that was too steep for the wagons to descend. The teamsters cleared trees to make a roadway down the five-hundred-foot slope. Then they tied a one-hundred-foot rope on the back axle of the wagon and took two loops around a large tree. Several men held on to the rope and eased the wagon down. When they reached the end of the rope, they secured the wagon with short rope. They repeated the process with the long rope until the wagon reached the bottom. George and his dog rode in one of the wagons when it made its almost vertical descent.

That afternoon, the entourage passed Alum Creek and met Howard's command at Mud Springs. After remaining there for a day, the party moved to the Lower Falls of the Yellowstone.

Below the falls the roads were better, but the going was still slow; it took nine days to go eighteen miles. Arnold said, "Cowan suffered intensely, but bore it bravely. Part of the time he was standing on his head, and then again he would be on his feet. It was enough to make a well man sick."[36]

Later the party had a scare when teamsters reported seeing seventy-five Indians on the mountains. Arnold told George he would reconnoiter and if the Indians were coming they would hide in the brush. It turned out the Indians were Crows under the command of Lieutenant Gustavus Doane from Fort Ellis and were looking for General Howard.

While the party waited, heavy rains made it impossible to keep George's underwear dry. George sent to Captain Spurgeon, the supply officer, and asked to buy some underwear. Spurgeon said he could not get to his supply, but a man who was with him said the boxes were open and the captain could get to things easily. According to Arnold, "This was a fair sample of Howard's noble-hearted officers. Noble, valorous Captain Spurgeon. As soon as he reached Fort Ellis he got uproariously drunk over his great achievements."[37]

Arnold said he and George later encountered "a different lot of soldiers, Lieutenants Doane and Scott, who were very kind, and willing to do anything that would be of benefit to anyone in want. We certainly needed their kind assistance,"[38] because the rain continued nearly all the way to Fort Ellis.

When the party got to Bottlers Ranch in the Paradise Valley, George was too weak to stand. He had been in a wagon for three weeks jostling over the brand-new roads hacked from the rugged wilderness. Only his friend Arnold was there to tend his three gunshot wounds, and his dog, Dido, to offer consolation. Word was sent to Bozeman to let George's wife, Emma, know he was waiting for her there.

* * * *

Stereopticon view of Nez Perce refugees taken on August 30, 1877, at Bottlers Ranch five days after the Nez Perce release of Emma Cowan and her siblings. Front row from left: Ida Carpenter, Emma Cowan, and Frank Carpenter. Back row, members of Texas Jack Omohundro Party: Boney Ernest, Texas Jack Omohundro, Captain Baily, and T. B. Birmingham.

MONTANA HISTORICAL SOCIETY PHOTO BY CALFEE AND CATLIN

The image of blood gushing from George's head must have haunted Emma while she waited at her parents' ranch near Radersburg for news from her brother. Frank had returned to the park to look for George, and Emma knew he would rush to tell her if there was any news.

General Howard's army had entered the park, and news kept trickling back that soldiers had found other members of the Radersburg Party alive. That let Emma cling to the hope that her husband had survived.

Emma had been home for a week when two men arrived at her father's house. She invited them in, but they refused to enter, so she talked to them at the door. For several minutes, they discussed what Emma described as "ordinary subjects."

Then one of the men handed her an extra edition of the *Helena Independent*. The newspaper headline screamed, "Cowan Alive. He Is with Howard's Command."[39]

The story read: "Two scouts just in from Howard's command say that George is with Howard and is doing well and will recover. He is shot through the thigh and the side and wounded in the head. Howard was 14 miles this side of Yellowstone Lake."[40]

The news hit Emma so hard that she had to sit down on the doorstep to regain her composure. Then the men told her that George was badly wounded, but he would live. They didn't know the answer to Emma's most urgent question: Would Howard send George back by Henrys Lake to Virginia City, or take him through the park and then send him to Bozeman? She desperately wanted to be by George's side, but she didn't know where to meet him. Virginia City and Bozeman were in opposite directions from Radersburg.

Later, Emma said her brother, Frank Carpenter, arrived, but he couldn't add anything. Time dragged at the ranch house. Finally, Emma decided to go to Helena to wait for news near the telegraph office. A whole week passed. Then at 10 p.m. on Saturday night, Emma received the long-awaited telegram. It said George would be brought to Bozeman the next day.

Emma didn't even wait for daylight. By 3 a.m. she was rushing up the Missouri Valley toward Bozeman, where she arrived at 9 p.m. She had made the 125-mile trip in just fifteen hours. Normally it took three days.

But George wasn't in Bozeman. He had given out at Bottlers Ranch and was waiting for Emma there.

Emma gulped down supper at a Bozeman hotel, rented a team and double-seated carriage, and was back on the road by 10 p.m. Three miles east of Bozeman, she passed Fort Ellis, but the military post was nearly empty. The cavalry stationed there were scattered across the country trying to find the Nez Perce and contain them in Yellowstone Park.

Soon, Emma entered Rocky Canyon where a new road had been carved into the hillside. The full moon over the perpendicular limestone cliffs that towered above the road must have cast ominous shadows as Emma raced along. About seven miles east of Bozeman, she turned south and headed over Trail Creek Pass through another narrow canyon.

The sun was shining when she came down Trail Creek into the Paradise Valley of the Yellowstone River. By 10 a.m., Emma arrived at Bottlers. In just thirty-one hours, she had traveled 175 miles over rough roads by team and wagon to be with her husband.

People at Bottlers were coy in their descriptions of the Cowans' reunion. One of them put it this way: "The meeting of Cowan and his wife can better be imagined than described. Their joy was too sacred for public perusal."[41]

George felt strong enough to travel and insisted on heading home immediately, so Emma arranged robes and blankets in the back of the carriage she had rented and made him comfortable there. Emma sat in the back seat to be near George. Arnold, who had been in the wagon with George clear through the park, sat in front with the driver.

By late afternoon, they crossed Trail Creek Pass and came down a road carved into the side of Rocky Canyon about seven miles east of Bozeman. They were admiring the view when a harness strap broke. The carriage tongue rammed into the ground, flipping the vehicle. Luckily, the carriage seats weren't fastened, so the passengers were thrown clear. They found themselves in a pile of seats, robes, and blankets on the hillside. The carriage flew through the air and tumbled down the hill, landing bottom side up three hundred feet below.

George's companions arranged the blankets and robes beside the road and made a new nest for him. When they placed him in it, they discovered his wounds were bleeding again. They built a fire, heated some water, and bound them again.

Soon, a rider leading a pack animal approached. The driver borrowed a horse and dashed to Fort Ellis to get help from the soldiers there. Two hours later he returned with an ambulance.

A crowd was waiting in the street when the ambulance arrived in Bozeman. George was carried into a hotel, where Arnold began tending his freshly opened wounds. When Arnold sat down to reach George, the bed collapsed. The fall jolted him hard, but he joked that "if we couldn't kill him any other way, to turn the artillery loose on him."[42]

That evening, George's faithful dog Dido crawled into bed with him and had her puppies.

ACKNOWLEDGMENTS

Many people assisted in the preparation of this book. I am grateful to Humanities Montana, which provided motivation by including me in their impressive speakers bureau. Too many people to name helped me, but I want to list a few. Ann Butterfield read chapter drafts and offered pointed criticism and unflagging encouragement. Ralph Schmidt used his formidable knowledge and sharp eye to catch errors that the less astute would have missed. Craig Lancaster suggested many ways to refine the writing and make additions to provide context. Ken Egan took time from his busy schedule as executive director of Humanities Montana to read a draft and offer insightful suggestions. Rachel Phillips, research coordination at the Gallatin History Museum, graciously shared her knowledge of the museum collection and helped me select photographs. I thank these—and other people—for their bounteous encouragement. They made the book better. Of course, I take full responsibility for any remaining errors.

Endnotes

Chapter 1: The Magnetic Cabin
1 *The last outpost of civilization* Dunraven 1976, p. 207.

Chapter 2: General Sherman's Trip
1 Sherman's letter is reproduced in the *New Northwest,* July 6, 1877.
2 *We saw only four buffaloes* Sherman 1878, p. 31.
3 *I now regard the Sioux Indian problem* Sherman 1878, p. 28.
4 *With this post occupied* Sherman 1878, p. 29.
5 *Governor Potts and most of the volunteers* Greene 2000, p. 111.
6 *I do not suppose* Sherman 1878, p. 33.
7 *From Mount Washburn* Sherman 1878, p. 35.
8 *The real object and aim* Sherman August 9, 1878.
9 *The meager details* Poe 1878, p. 81.

Chapter 3: Radersburg to Geyserland
1 *The hot, dry weather* Cowan 1908. Huge swarms of Rock Mountain locusts that spread across the American plains were recorded beginning in 1870. The species apparently was extinct by about 1900.
2 *I enjoyed beyond measure* Cowan 1908, p. 151.
3 *We were very fortunate* Cowan 1908, p. 154.
4 *My fairy books* Cowan 1908, p. 154.
5 *As I grew older* Cowan 1908, p. 154.
6 *We found an acquaintance* Cowan 1908, p. 155.
7 *You must see them for yourself* Cowan 1908, p. 158.
8 *She would be so much company* Cowan 1908, p. 160.
9 *provisions, tents, guns* Cowan 1908, p. 161.
10 *Bird, because she was trim* Cowan 1908, p. 161.
11 *trying to skin a cat* Carpenter 1878, p. 9.
12 *Newspapers that would have come to Sterling* e.g., *Bozeman Avant Courier*, August 2, 1877; *Helena Weekly Herald*, August 2, 1877.
13 *When the next morning came* Cowan 1908, p. 161.
14 *Men on horseback* A paved road now passes through the canyon by the lake formed by an earthquake in 1959.
15 *Sawtell built a veritable village* Early Yellowstone tourist Calvin Clawson described Sawtell's compound in 1871. Clawson 2003.
16 *Dingee declared the circus closed* Carpenter 1878, p. 14.
17 *We picked an immense quantity* Carpenter 1878, p. 15.
18 *Anybody could do it* Carpenter 1878, p. 16.

131

19 *We stood in awe* Carpenter 1878, p. 16.
20 *The day, which had been lovely* Cowan 1908, p. 99.
21 *They wanted to save* Cowan 1908, p. 99.
22 *We had a pleasant time* Carpenter 1878, p. 17.
23 *He sprang to his feet* Carpenter 1878, p. 18.
24 *Actually, waterfalls and cascades* Evermann 1896. Later fish were planted in the area and they are plentiful now.

Chapter 4: Scouts Search for the Nez Perce
1 *The scout refused* Redington 1932, p. 56.
2 *He said the Nez Perce were fighting* Duncan McDonald, *The New Northwest*, January 27, 1879.
3 *They covered the courthouse windows* Barrett undated.
4 *the first written description* Herendeen's account of the Bighorn Battle was published in the July 8, 1876, issue of the *Helena Herald*.
5 *Bean had been in charge* Bean undated.
6 *I was getting tired* Bean undated.
7 *That settles it* Bean undated.
8 *As we saw signal fires* Bean undated.
9 *We seen them pack up* Bean undated.
10 *As they hurried* Bean said the miners were from Butte, but two other accounts say they were from Pony. Topping 1883, p. 212; *Avant Courier*, August 30, 1877.
11 *We told them where the Indian camp* Bean undated.
12 *They had fine fat ponies* Bean undated.
13 *The guard fired once* Bean undated.
14 *had gone out to shear* Topping 1883, p. 212.
15 *Indians were camped* *Avant Courier*, August 30, 1877.
16 *We had all the scouting* Bean undated.

Chapter 5: The Reluctant Guide
1 *After he crossed Mary Mountain* Carpenter 1878, p. 37.
2 *the world's largest geyser* The Excelsior Geyser was active in the 1880s when it erupted several times, throwing a column of water three hundred feet wide and three hundred feet into the air. It was mostly inactive until 1985 when it had eruptions up to 120 feet, according to Whittlesey 2006, p. 101.
3 *You are not Sioux* New Northwest, September 14, 1877.
4 *hyas skukum tum tum* New Northwest, September 14, 1877.
5 *a man called Joe Hale* Called Poker Joe hereafter.
6 *Soon Poker Joe brought Ida's sister Emma* Cowan 1908, p. 174.
7 *Through this terrible ordeal* New Northwest, September 14, 1877.
8 *a white man surrounded* Carpenter 1878, pp. 98–99.
9 *Shively said Irwin was wearing* Guie and McWhorter 1935, p. 260.
10 *the Indians learned about the other tourists* Carpenter 1878, pp. 98–99.

11 *If you try New Northwest*, September 14, 1877.
12 *intended to release Shively* McDonald *New Northwest*, February 7, 1878.

Chapter 6: Frolic in Geyserland

1 *wild with the eagerness of seeing all things* Cowan 1908, p. 164.
2 *appearance of a large manufacturing town* Carpenter 1878, p. 23.
3 *We had realized our expectations* Cowan 1908, p. 165.
4 *thumping and pumping brimstone* Carpenter 1878, p. 26.
5 *found hundreds of well-preserved names* Carpenter 1878, p. 28.
6 *Yes, damn you* Carpenter 1878, p. 28.
7 *The first we had heard about it* Carpenter 1878, p. 28.
8 *erroneously attributed* Cowan 1908, p. 166.
9 *would come in just sixty-five minutes* Intervals between Old Faithful's eruptions have lengthened over time. In 2018 they were about ninety minutes.
10 *the earth would be rent asunder* Cowan 1908, p. 165.
11 *most strikingly beautiful views* Carpenter 1878, p. 32.
12 *clean as a Chinaman could wash it* Carpenter 1878, p. 34.
13 *Off she goes* Carpenter 1878, p. 35.
14 *Old Faithful seems to have been angered* Carpenter 1878, p. 35.
15 *wretched looking specimen of humanity* Carpenter 1878, p. 38.
16 *passed Mud Geyser* Mud geyser is now a quiet, bubbling hot spring. Whittlesey 2006, p. 182.
17 *sear the skin like hot sealing wax* The feature is now dormant.
18 *looks like a huge mirror* Carpenter 1878, p. 40.
19 *one prolonged sulfurous oath* Carpenter 1878, p. 40.
20 *General Sherman and party* Cowan 1908, p. 166.
21 *the day before the Nez Perce arrived Avant Courier*, August 27, 1877.
22 *We felt somewhat depressed* Cowan 1908, p. 166.
23 *his party preferred being elsewhere* Cowan 1908, p. 166.
24 *dressed up as brigands* Cowan 1908, p. 166.
25 *Al Oldham, with his swart complexion* Cowan 1908, p. 166.
26 *They made the woods ring* Cowan 1908, p. 166.
27 *We better not go there* McWhorter 2000, p. 173.

Chapter 7: Radersburg Capture

1 *They covered the courthouse windows* Barrett undated.
2 *the point where Nez Perce Creek flowed* The stream wasn't called Nez Perce Creek until after the events of 1877. Frank Carpenter referred to it as "the East Fork of the Firehole."
3 *These people are not soldiers* McWhorter 2000, p. 173.
4 *No, we will capture them* McWhorter 2000, p. 173.
5 *walked into the camp and greeted Dingee* Dialogue is from Carpenter 1878, p. 54 ff. It is doubtful that use of pidgin English renders the Nez Perce speech patterns accurately.

6 *That is Joseph's voice Helena Weekly Herald*, September 6, 1877.

7 *this materially lessened his chance* Cowan 1908, p. 167.

8 *which could have only ended disastrously* Cowan 1908, p. 167. In his book (Carpenter 1878, p. 58) Frank Carpenter reports that the tourists were well armed with rifles, revolvers, a shotgun, and more than two hundred rounds of ammunition. George Cowan concurred with his wife that the party had limited ammunition (Guie and McWhorter 1935, p. 254). In any case, the Radersburg Party wouldn't have stood a chance against the Nez Perce, who outnumbered them about thirty to one.

9 *Me Charley* The dialogue is from Frank Carpenter's 1878 book. Doubtless he reconstructed it.

10 *Joseph's Injuns come up here, kill you* In his book, Frank Carpenter frequently implies that members of Chief Joseph's band were more hostile than those of other bands. Other accounts don't corroborate this.

11 *We could see about three miles of Indians* Carpenter 1878, p. 58.

12 *glinted on the polished surface of the gun barrels* Cowan 1908, p. 103.

13 *The Indians pretended all the while* Cowan 1908, p. 168.

14 *the Indians seemed to enjoy the "confiscated property"* Cowan 1908, p. 168.

15 *Frank decided to ride ahead* Frank Carpenter wrote two versions of his trip to the head of the Indian caravan and his conversation with Poker Joe, who he misidentified as White Bird. The account here is based on Carpenter's letter to the *Helena Weekly Herald*, which was published September 13, 1877. In his book, which was published a year later, Carpenter says Poker Joe told him he needed to confer with chiefs Looking Glass and Joseph before he could say if the tourists could go home. The book version appears to be highly embellished, so the newspaper account is relied upon here.

16 *The Indians seemed friendly* Cowan 1908, p. 170.

17 *You had better get out of here Helena Weekly Herald*, September 6, 1877.

18 *You get'm in woods* Arnold in Carpenter 1878, p. 150.

19 *Get'm horses quick* Carpenter 1878, p. 68.

20 *Where balance of party?* Carpenter 1878, p. 70.

21 *Had I have shot him* Oldham in Carpenter 1878, p. 137.

22 *It was lively times* Oldham in Carpenter 1878, p. 137.

23 *Where are you hurt?* G. Cowan in Carpenter 1878, p. 136.

24 *Be brave, keep up* G. Cowan in Carpenter 1878, p. 142.

25 *The holes in those gun barrels* Cowan 1903, p. 173.

26 *Kill me first* G. Cowan in Carpenter 1878, p. 142.

27 *the horror of it all* Cowan 1903, p. 173.

28 *he heard intermittent gunfire New Northwest*, September 14, 1877.

CHAPTER 8: JOE ROBERTS'S ADVENTURE

1 *a slim supper* Weikert 1900, p. 154.

2 *the general hurried back* General Sherman's aide-de-camp Colonel O. M. Poe describes the meeting and exchange of information, although Weikert makes no mention of meeting the famous general in his account of the Helena Party's trip.

3 *ought to be shut up* Weikert 1900, p. 157.

4 *a damned big party of tourists* Stone 1877. *Avant Courier*, September 6, 1877.
5 *Your elk* Stone 1877. *Avant Courier*, September 6, 1877.
6 *We could see something alive* Stone 1877. *Avant Courier*, September 6, 1877.
7 *My God, it's Indians* Stone 1877. *Avant Courier*, September 6, 1877.
8 *a perfect hiding place* The campsite is described in Brown 1967.
9 *I'm murdered* Stewart 1877. *Avant Courier*, September 27, 1877.

CHAPTER 9: A DECENT BURIAL

1 *whoop them up* Weikert 1900, p. 159.
2 *made our hair raise* Weikert 1900, p. 159.
3 *I was perfectly cool* Weikert 1900, p. 161.
4 *splintered my shoulder* Weikert 1900, p. 161.
5 *turn my old repeater loose* Weikert 1900, p. 161.
6 *I up and let them have one* Weikert 1900, p. 161.
7 *Oh Andy, let me ride* Weikert 1900, p. 167.
8 *it seemed that long* Weikert 1900, p. 167.
9 *I returned sad at heart* Weikert 1900, p. 167.
10 *What will Mrs. Roberts say* Avant Courier, September 6, 1877.
11 *you will give me a decent burial* Weikert 1900, p. 168.
12 *I told him jestingly* Weikert 1900, p. 168.
13 *we had better go on* Weikert 1900, p. 170.
14 *how we were fixed* Weikert 1900, p. 170.
15 *Eighteen guns kept up* Weikert 1900, p. 170.
16 *They kept pouring lead* Weikert 1900, p. 170.
17 *Goodbye, Toby* Weikert 1900, p. 170.
18 *They were terrible brave* Weikert 1900, p. 171.
19 *I flopped myself down* Weikert 1900, p. 173.
20 *We rounded a point* Scott 1928, p. 61.
21 *He is nothing but a killer* McWhorter 2000, p. 177.
22 *God bless you, Andy* Weikert 1900, p. 173.

CHAPTER 10: CAPTIVITY AND RELEASE

1 *I could see nothing* Cowan 1908, p. 174.
2 *You Injun now* Carpenter 1878, p. 83.
3 *of the death of the boys* Carpenter 1878, p. 84.
4 *Emma, don't you know me* Carpenter 1878, p. 85.
5 *I thought it to be an Indian* Cowan 1908, p. 172.
6 *The "noble red man"* Cowan 1908, p. 173.
7 *I glanced at the chief* Cowan 1908, p. 173.
8 *Such a forlorn child* Cowan 1908, p. 176.
9 *I was benumbed* Ida Carpenter in Carpenter 1878, p. 160.
10 *had the satisfaction of biting* in Carpenter 1878, p. 160.
11 *I rejoiced now* Ida Carpenter in Carpenter 1878, p. 161.

12 *I did not know* Ida Carpenter in Carpenter 1878, p. 161.
13 *I had read of savages* Ida Carpenter in Carpenter 1878, p. 161.
14 *The tea was so bitter* Ida Carpenter in Carpenter 1878, p. 162.
15 *Oh, how I rejoiced* Ida Carpenter in Carpenter 1878, p. 162.
16 *The formality of cleaning* Cowan 1908, p. 175.
17 *eyes were dim with tears* Cowan 1908, p. 176.
18 *We may be intercepted* Cowan 1908, p. 176.
19 *Something tells me* Cowan 1908, p. 176.
20 *All night. All Day.* Cowan 1908, p. 176.
21 *Me want you to tell'm* Carpenter 1878, p.109.
22 *I thought he would never stop* Guie and McWhorter 1935, p. 262.
23 *Maybe sometime soldiers catch'm* Carpenter 1878, p. 110.
24 *My friend* Carpenter 1878, p. 110.
25 *If I had known it Helena Weekly Herald*, September 13, 1877.
26 *We dared not retrace that route* Cowan 1908, p. 177.
27 *falls coming from the snow* Carpenter 1878, p. 118.
28 *We cannot be far* Carpenter 1878, p. 118.
29 *We are safe* Carpenter 1878, p. 120.
30 *How are you, Lieutenant* Carpenter 1878, p. 121.
31 *How are you, sir?* Carpenter 1878, p. 121.
32 *Got anything to eat?* Carpenter 1878, p. 121.
33 *Who are those young ladies* Carpenter 1878, p. 121.
34 *We are all that is left* Carpenter 1878, p. 121.
35 *That's none of our party* Carpenter 1878, p. 122.
36 *Are you one of the Helena Party?* Carpenter 1878, p. 122.
37 *Yes, my name is Pfister* Carpenter 1878, p. 123.
38 *the National Park Massacres Bozeman Avant Courier*, August 30, 1877.
39 *he never found a time* Cowan 1908, p. 179.
40 *Roll out and let us in* Carpenter 1878, p. 126.
41 *I'll go back* Carpenter, 1878, p. 127.
42 *The news relieved our anxiety* Carpenter 1878, p. 127.
43 *a somewhat amusing incident* Cowan 1908, p. 179.
44 *They examined the stirrup* Cowan 1908, p. 179.
45 *I protected the rear* Cowan 1908, p. 180.
46 *Neither Emma nor Frank recalled New York Sun*, October 22, 1877.
47 *took advantage of the fact* Cowan 1908, p. 180.
48 *bogus 50-cent pair* Guie and McWhorter 1935, p. 264.
49 *We retired again* Cowan 1908, p. 180.
50 *On the way they met* Estimates vary on the number of Crow accompanying Doane.
51 *Those reports with headlines Helena Weekly Herald*, September 6, 1877.

CHAPTER 11: BEN STONE ESCAPES
1 *A lookout on the top of the hill* The campsite is described in Brown 1967, p. 328.
2 *should be thinking of his girl* Stone 1877. *Avant Courier*, September 6, 1877.

3 *Ben, you're gassing* Stone 1877. *Avant Courier*, September 6, 1877.

4 *Now tell me, Ben* Stone 1877. *Avant Courier*, September 6, 1877.

5 *I'm a goner* Stone 1877. *Avant Courier*, September 6, 1877.

6 *pretty good grub* Stone 1877. *Avant Courier*, September 6, 1877.

7 *I have been waiting for you* Stone 1877. *Avant Courier*, September 6, 1877.

8 *My God, Ben* Stone 1877. *Avant Courier*, September 6, 1877.

9 *Thank God for that* Stone 1877. *Avant Courier*, September 6, 1877.

10 *Let's travel lively* Stone 1877. *Avant Courier*, September 6, 1877.

11 *I am murdered* Stewart 1877. *Avant Courier*, September 27, 1877.

12 *I have a little* Stewart 1877. *Avant Courier*, September 27, 1877.

13 *refreshed me considerably* Stewart 1877. *Avant Courier*, September 27, 1877.

14 *acted just as if she wanted* Stewart 1877. *Avant Courier*, September 27, 1877.

15 *Thank God! Here comes Wilkie* Stone 1877. *Avant Courier*, September 6, 1877.

16 *grub was getting scarce* Stone 1877. *Avant Courier*, September 6, 1877.

17 *I've caught something else* Stone 1877. *Avant Courier*, September 6, 1877.

18 *Andy and McCartney have found* Stone 1877. *Avant Courier*, September 6, 1877.

19 *We had better cache ourselves* Stone 1877. *Avant Courier*, September 6, 1877.

20 *I'll warn him* Stone 1877. *Avant Courier*, September 6, 1877.

21 *Good boy, Jake* Stone 1877. *Avant Courier*, September 6, 1877.

22 *Who goes there* This exchange is from Stone 1877. *Avant Courier*, September 6, 1877.

23 *Here is the colored man* Stone 1877. *Avant Courier*, September 6, 1877.

CHAPTER 12: GEORGE'S ORDEAL

1 *I must have lain* George Cowan in Carpenter 1878, p. 144.

2 *I supposed my wife* George Cowan in Carpenter 1878, p. 144.

3 *I supposed then that I would die* George Cowan in Carpenter 1878, p. 145.

4 *The pleasure of the meeting* George Cowan in Carpenter 1878, p. 146.

5 *I grasped her by the neck* George Cowan in Carpenter 1878, p. 146.

6 *I soon had some excellent hot coffee* George Cowan in Carpenter 1878, p. 146.

7 *I could, as a last resort* George Cowan in Carpenter 1878, p. 146.

8 *I shudder now* George Cowan in Carpenter 1878, p. 146.

9 *hailed with pleasure* George Cowan in Carpenter 1878, p. 146.

10 *gave myself up for dead* George Cowan in Carpenter 1878, p. 147.

11 *S. G. Fisher and J. W. Reddington* Guie and McWhorter 1935, p. 266.

12 *It seems the spirit of revenge* George Cowan in Carpenter 1878, p. 147.

13 *My wife* George Cowan in Carpenter 1878, p. 148.

14 *No news yet* George Cowan in Carpenter 1878, p. 148.

15 *How far are the Indians* Arnold in Carpenter 1878, p. 153.

16 *About seventy-five miles* Arnold in Carpenter 1878, p. 153.

17 *We do not want* Arnold in Carpenter 1878, p. 153.

18 *I am going back* Arnold in Carpenter 1878, p. 154.

19 *What were you doing* Arnold in Carpenter 1878, p. 154.

20 *So should General Sherman* Arnold in Carpenter 1878, p. 154.

21 *George was a most pitiful object* Arnold in Carpenter 1878, p. 154.

22 *I cannot thank any of Howard's surgeons* George Cowan in Carpenter 1878, p. 148.
23 *in a manner not in keeping* Arnold in Carpenter 1878, p. 155.
24 *What's wrong with the fellow?* Guie and McWhorter 1935, p. 268.
25 *If you were in his place* Guie and McWhorter 1935, p. 268.
26 *Why, I just came from Bozeman* Guie and McWhorter 1935, p. 268.
27 *Now you see here* Guie and McWhorter 1935, p. 268.
28 *Before I was despondent* George Cowan in Carpenter 1878, p. 149.
29 *The treatment that he received* Arnold in Carpenter 1878, p. 155.
30 *There would not have been an officer* Arnold in Carpenter 1878, p. 155.
31 *I supposed Sherman was "prospecting or trapping"* Arnold in Carpenter 1878, p. 155.
32 *We gathered up what we could* Arnold in Carpenter 1878, p. 155.
33 *We, who were left behind* Arnold in Carpenter 1878, p. 155.
34 *What you say may be true* Howard 1881, p. 244.
35 *Henry Buck, a teamster* Buck 1922, pp. 83–84.
36 *Cowan suffered intensely* Arnold in Carpenter 1878, p. 156.
37 *This was a fair sample* Arnold in Carpenter 1878, p. 157.
38 *A different lot of soldiers* Arnold in Carpenter 1878, p. 157.
39 *Cowan Alive* Guie and McWhorter 1935, p. 305.
40 *Two scouts just in* Guie and McWhorter 1935, p. 305.
41 *The meeting of Cowan* Carpenter 1878, p. 158.
42 *if we couldn't kill him* Arnold in Carpenter 1878, p. 158.

References

Books and Manuscripts

Barrett, Alice, undated manuscript. Montana Historical Society, Small Collection 400.

Bean, Jack, *Real Hunting Tales*. Undated reminiscence. Gallatin History Museum, Bozeman, Montana.

Brown, Mark H., *The Flight of the Nez Perce*. Lincoln, University of Nebraska Press 1967.

Buck, Henry S., *The Story of the Nez Perce Indian Campaign during the Summer of 1877*. SC 492 Montana Historical Society Archives, Helena, Montana 1922.

Bullock, Seth, *A Memorable Trip to Yellowstone National Park from Helena*. Montana Historical Society Archives, Helena, Montana 1872.

Carpenter, Frank D., *The Wonders of Geyserland: A Trip to the Yellowstone National Park of Wyoming*. Black Earth, Wisconsin, Burnett & Son, Printers and Publishers 1878.

Chief Joseph, "An Indian's Views of Indian Affairs," *North American Review*, Vol. 128 (April 1879): 412–33.

Clawson, Calvin C., *A Ride to the Infernal Regions: Yellowstone's First Tourists* (edited by Eugene Lee Silliman). Helena, Montana, Riverbend Publishing 2003.

Cook, Charles W., David E. Folsom, and William Peterson, *The Valley of the Upper Yellowstone* (edited by Aubry L. Haines). Norman, University of Oklahoma Press 1965.

Cowan, Mrs. George F. [Emma], "Reminiscences of a Pioneer Life," *Contributions to the Historical Society of Montana* Vol. 4 (1908): 156–87.

DeLacy, Walter W., "A Trip up the South Snake River in 1863," *Contributions to the Historical Society of Montana* Vol. 1 (1876): 100–27.

Doane, Gustavus C., *Report of Lieutenant Gustavus C. Doane upon the So-Called Yellowstone Expedition of 1870* (41st Cong., 34d Sess; Senate Exec. Doc. 51.). Washington, DC, Govt. Printing Office 1871.

Dunraven, The Earl of, *The Great Divide: Travels in the Upper Yellowstone in the Summer of 1874*. Lincoln, University of Nebraska 1976.

Evermann, Barton Warren, "Two Ocean Pass," *Inland Educator* 2:6 (July 1896): 299–306.

Everts, Truman, "Thirty-Seven Days of Peril," *Scribner's Monthly* 3 (November 1871): 1–17.

Folsom, David E., "The Folsom-Cook Explorations of the Upper Yellowstone in the Year 1869," *Contributions to the Historical Society of Montana* Vol. 5 (1904): 349–69.

Greene, Jerome A., *Nez Perce Summer 1877*. Helena, Montana, Montana Historical Society Press., 2000.

Guie, Hester Dean, and Lucullus Virgil McWhorter, *Adventures in Geyserland: The Wonders of Geyserland Edition 1878 by Frank D. Carpenter*. Caldwell, Idaho, Caxton Printers 1935.

Gunnison, J. W., *A History of the Mormons*. Philadelphia: Lippincott, Grambo & Co. 1852.

Haines, Aubrey L., *Yellowstone National Park: Its Exploration and Establishment*. Washington, U.S. Department of Interior 1974.

Haines, Aubrey L., *The Yellowstone Story: History of Our First National Park*. Denver, University Press of Colorado 1996 (revised).

Hartman, Kelly Suzanne, *A Brief History of Cook City*. Charleston, The History Press 2019.

Howard, Oliver Otis, *Nez Perce Joseph*. Boston, Lee and Shepard Publishers 1881.

Langford, Nathaniel P., "Wonders of the Yellowstone," *Scribner's Monthly* 2 (May–June 1871): 113–28.

Langford, Nathaniel P., *Vigilante Days and Ways*. Boston, J. C. Cupples Co. 1890.

Langford, Nathaniel P., *The Discovery of Yellowstone Park*. F. J. Haynes 1905.

McWhorter, Lucullus Virgil, *Yellow Wolf: His Own Story*. Caldwell, Idaho, Caxton Press 2000.

Poe, O. M., "From Fort Ellis to the Yellowstone National Park and Return to Fort Ellis," pages 70-83 in Generals P. H. Sheridan and W. T. Sherman, *Report of the Inspection Made in the Summer of 1877*. Washington, U.S. Government Printing Office, 1877.

Raynolds, W. F., *Exploration of the Yellowstone*. Washington, U.S. Government Printing Office 1868.

Redington, John W., "Scouting in Montana in the 1870s," *Frontier* 13:1 (November 1932): 55–68.

Russell, Osborne, *Journal of a Trapper, or, Nine Years in the Rocky Mountains, 1834–1843*. Boise, Idaho, Sims-York Co. 1914.

Schullery, Paul, "Yellowstone's Ecological Holocaust," *Montana: The Magazine of Western History* Vol. 4 (Autumn 1997): 16–22.

Schullery, Paul, and Lee Whittlesey, *Myth and History in the Creation of Yellowstone National Park*. Lincoln: University of Nebraska Press 2000.

Scott, Hugh Lenox, *Some Memories of a Soldier*. New York, The Century Co. 1928.

Sherman, William T., *Reports of Inspection Made in the Summer of 1877, Generals P. H. Sheridan and W. T. Sherman*. Washington, U.S. Government Printing Office 1878.

Strong, W. E., *A Trip to the Yellowstone National Park in July, August, and September, 1875*. Norman: University of Oklahoma Press 1868.

Topping, E. S., *Chronicles of the Yellowstone*. Saint Paul, Pioneer Press 1883.

Tracy, Sarah Jane, "Reminiscences of a Trip through Yellowstone Park in 1874." Undated manuscript. Museum of the Rockies, Bozeman, Montana.

Trumbull, Walter, "The Washburn Yellowstone Expedition," *Overland Monthly* 6 (May–June 1871): 431–37, 489–96.

Victor, Francis Fuller, *The River of the West*. San Francisco, R. W. Bliss & Company, 1870.

Weikert, Andrew J., "Journal of the Tour through the Yellowstone National Park in August and September 1877," *Contributions to the Historical Society of Montana* Vol. 3 (1900): 153–74.

Wheeler, Olin D., "Nathaniel Pitt Langford: The Vigilante, the Explorers, the Expounder and First Superintendent of the Yellowstone Park," *Collections of the Minnesota Historical Society* Vol. 15 (1915): 631–68.

Whittlesey, Lee H., *Yellowstone Place Names* (second edition). Wonderland Publishing Company 2006.

NEWSPAPERS

Avant Courier, Bozeman, Montana

Helena Weekly Herald, Helena, Montana

The New Northwest, Deer Lodge, Montana

Index

Alum Creek: Cowan, G., at, 126; Radersburg Party at, 53

Arnold, A. J., ix, 17, 23, 50; capture of, 59–60; Cowan, G., and, 121–22, 123, 126, 129; at Henrys Lake, 121; at Lake Yellowstone, 52; Poker Joe and, 63–64; Sherman, W., and, 123

Arsenic Springs, 51

Baily (Captain), *127*

Bannack, 30, 57

Bannock Indians, 68; Fisher and, 63; with Howard, 29, 125

Barlow (topographer), 10–11

Baronett's Bridge, 43; Sherman, T., at, 11

Battle of Big Hole River. *See* Big Hole River

Battle of Bear Paws, xxi; Poker Joe at, 98

Battle of the Little Bighorn, 5; Cheyenne at, 101; Herendeen and, xi, 30–31; Montana Column at, 31; Sioux at, 101

Bean, Jack, xi, *32*; at Gallatin River, 33; Gibbon and, 31, 36; at Henrys Lake, 33–35; in Virginia City, 35–36

Bear Paws. *See* Battle of Bear Paws

Beehive Geyser, 10

Big Hole River: Cowan, E., and, 54; Gibbon at, xxi, 2, 11–13, 30, 70, 101; Nez Perce at, xviii, xxi, 2, 8, 11–13, 21, 29, 30, 47, 69; Poker Joe and, 57

Bighorn Mountains, 37

Bighorn River, 7

Birmingham, T. B., *127*

Bitterroot Valley, 7–8, 12, 21

Bottler, Frederick, 9–10

Bottlers Ranch, *9*, 9–10; Cowan, G., at, 126, 129; Radersburg Party at, 106, *127*

Bozeman, 57, 84; Cowan, E., in, 123, 126; Radersburg Party to, 97–98; Stone to, 115; Weikert to, 89

Bozeman Pass, 7

Buck, Henry, xiii, 124, 125

buffalo, 6; in Montana, 7, 68

Bureau of Indian Affairs, 6

Calfee, Henry "Bird," 105, 106

Carpenter, Frank, ix, xxii, 17, *18*, 20–22, 26; at Bottlers Ranch, *127*; as captive, 41; capture and release of, 60–61, 92–107; Cowan, E., and, 93–94, 123; Cowan, G., and, 119, 123; Helena Party and, 98, 99–101; to McCartney's cabin, 83; Meyers and, 46–47; Poker Joe and, 64, 97–98, 99, 134n15; shooting and death of, 95

Carpenter, Ida, ix, *18*, 20, 22, 44; at Bottlers Ranch, *127*; capture and release of, 60–61, 94–107; Cowan, E., and, 94–95, 96, 97, 123; Cowan, G., and, 94–95, 123; laundry in geyser by, 49; at Lower Geyser Basin, 55; to McCartney's cabin, 83; Poker Joe and, 94

Cascade Creek, 111

Castle Geyser: Radersburg Party at, 48, 49; Sherman, W., at, 10

cattle, 50–51

Cheyenne, xviii; at Battle of the Little Bighorn, 101; Montana Column and, 31; to reservations, 31

Christianity, xix

Clarks Fork Mines, 11, 43, 83

Clematis Gulch, 1

Cody, Buffalo Bill, xiii, 2; gold and, 50; Omohundro and, 51

Cowan, Emma, ix, xiii, *15*, *18*, 21; at Bottlers Ranch, *127*, 129; capture and release of, 60–61, 92–107; Carpenter, F., and, 93–94; Carpenter, I., and, 94–95, 96, 97, 123; Cowan, G., and, 65–67, 123, 126–29; at Henrys Lake, 25; Joseph and, 93; laundry in geyser by, 49; at Lower Geyser Basin, 44–56; at Mammoth Hot Springs, 16–17; at McCartney's cabin, 3, 83; in Montana, 14; Poker Joe

and, 96, 97; Sherman, W., and, 54; Shively and, 97; at Tower Fall, *102*; in Virginia City, 14–16; in Yellowstone Park, 16–17, *66*

Cowan, George, ix, 14, 17, *18*; Arnold and, 121–22, 123, 126, 129; at Bottlers Ranch, 126, 129; Carpenter, F., and, 119, 123; Carpenter, I., and, 94–95; Cowan, E., and, 65–67, 123, 126–29; crawling by, 118, 120; dog of, 19, 25, 50, 119–20, 125–26, 129; on Firehole River, 120; at Henrys Lake, 25; Howard and, 121, 123, 124; at Lower Falls, 126; at Lower Geyser Basin, 44–56, 119–20, 122; Mann and, 119; ordeal of, 116–29; shooting of, 65–67, 103, 104, 116–18, *117*; in Yellowstone Park, *66*

Crow Indians, xviii, 40, 42, 68, 88; with Doane, 43, 107, 126; on reservations, 106

Custer, George Armstrong, xi, xxiii; Herendeen and, xi, 30–31; Sitting Bull and, xviii, 5. *See also* Battle of the Little Bighorn

Deadwood, 37

Deer Lodge: Gibbon at, 13, 30; Shively at, 43

Department of Columbia, 8

Department of Dakota, 8

Devil's Mud Pot, 45

The Devil's Well, 51

Dido (dog), 19, 25, 50, 119–20, 125–26, 129

Dietrich, Richard, x, 68–76, *73*, 74; burial of, 89–91; to Mammoth Hot Springs, 76; at McCartney's cabin, 83, 87, 88, 112; as music teacher, 79, *90*; Radersburg Party and, 105; Roberts and, 84; shooting and death of, xii, 43, 114; Weikert and, 83, 84, 89–91; Yellow Wolf and, 88–89

Dingee, William, ix, 17, 20, 22, 26, 45; capture of, 59–60; at Henrys Lake, 23–25, 121; at Lake Yellowstone, 52–53; laundry in geyser by, 49; at Lower Geyser Basin, 55; Poker Joe and, 63–64

Doane, Gustavus C., xi, 87–88; Crow Indians with, 43, 107, 126; from Fort Ellis, 126; at Henderson's Ranch, 89

Duncan, Leander, x, 70, *72*, 77; Radersburg Party and, 105; Stone and, 75–76

Dunraven, Earl of, 51

Emigrant Gulch, 10

Ennis, 21

Ernest, Boney, *127*

Excelsior Geyser, 39, 124, 132n2

Firehole River, 27; Cowan, G., on, 120; Excelsior geyser and, 39; Helena Party on, 42; Nez Perce Creek into, 62; Nez Perce on,

58; Radersburg Party on, 50, 62; Shively on, 38

Fisher, Stanton G., xi, 120; Bannock Indians and, 63

Fitzgerald (Doctor), 122

Flathead, 68

Foller, August, x, 70; Roberts and, 77–78, 115; to Virginia City, 89, 115

Fort Buford, 6

Fort Custer, 5

Fort Ellis, *31*; Doane from, 126; Irwin at, 97; Pfister to, 105; Radersburg Party and, 57; Schofield and, 103, 104, 105; scouts from, 30–36; Sherman, W., at, 7, 11–12, 70; Shively at, 43

Fort Fizzle, 8

Fort Missoula: Gibbons at, 12; Nez Perce and, 29

Fort Shaw, 12; Montana Column at, 31

Fountain Geyser, 3; Radersburg Party at, 45–46

Gallatin River, 19; Bean at, 33

Gallatin Valley, 13

Gardner River, 10; Helena Party on, 70, 84, 87

Gardner River Canyon, 104

geysers: Beehive, 10; Castle, 10, 48, 49; debris dumped into, 49; Excelsior, 39, 124, 132n2; Fountain Geyser, 3, 45–46; Giantess, 10, 48; laundry in, 49–50; Midway Geyser

Basin, 38; Mud, 41, 51; Old Faithful, 10–11, 47–49; specimen collecting from, 46; steam injuries from, 46–47. *See also* Lower Geyser Basin; Upper Geyser Basin

Giantess Geyser: Radersburg Party at, 48; Sherman, W., at, 10

Gibbon, John, xi, xviii, xxiii; Bean and, 31, 36; at Big Hole River, xxi, 2, 11–13, 30, 70, 101; at Deer Lodge, 13, 30; Department of Dakota and, 8; on Madison River, 27–28

gold, xix–xxi; in Bighorn Mountains, 37; Cody and, 50; Shively and, 37–38

Grand Prismatic Spring, 38–39

Gravelly Range, 21

The Great Divide (Dunraven), 51

Hale, Joe. *See* Poker Joe

Harmon, William, xiii, 54, 121

Hayden Valley, 98

Heap (topographer), 10–11

Helena Party, x–xi, 68–91, *72–73, 80*; Carpenter, F., and, 98, 99–101; on Firehole River, 42; on Gardner River, 70, 84, 87; horses of, 71, 80–81, 82, 85; at Lake Yellowstone, 80; at Mammoth Hot Springs, 4, 42, 70, 76–77, 82, 87, 111; at McCartney's cabin, 83, 87, 111–12; at Mount Washburn, 70, 83, 84; Nez Perce and, 4, 74–78; at Otter Creek, 80, 85; Radersburg Party and, 104–5; at Trail Creek

Pass, 11–12; at Yellowstone Falls, 70–71, 74, 75, 84. *See also specific members*

Henderson's Ranch, 11, 43; Doane at, 89; Helena Party to, 87; Nez Perce at, 88; Stone to, 113, 114

Henrys Fork, 30

Henrys Lake, 14–16, 21; Arnold at, 121; Bean and Herendeen at, 33–35; Dingee at, 23–25, 121; Howard at, 77, 121; Nez Perce at, 30, 33–35, 58; Radersburg Party at, 22–26, 62; to Virginia City, 22

Herendeen, George, xi, 30–31; at Gallatin River, 33; at Henrys Lake, 33–35

Hicks (prospector), 27

Horse Prairie, 26, 57

horses: of Helena Party, 71, 80–81, 82, 85; Nez Perce and, 29–30, 35, 42, 58, 92, 118–19; of Radersburg Party, 53, 55, 63; of Shively, 38; of Stewart, 110–11

Howard, Oliver Otis, xi, xiii, xviii, *xx*; Bannock Indians with, 29, 125; Baronett's Bridge and, 43; Cowan, G., and, 121, 123, 124; Department of Columbia and, 8; at Henrys Lake, 77, 121; Joseph and, xxii; at Mud Springs, 126; Nez Perce and, 69; *Nez Perce Joseph* by, xxii; peace council by, xxi; scout of, 29; scouts of, 120

Huston, George, xiii, 47–49, 51–53; to Mammoth Hot Springs, 53

Irwin, James, C., xiii, 41, 42, 101; at
    Fort Ellis, 97

Jefferson River, 19, 20
Joseph (Chief), xii, *18*; Cowan, E.,
    and, 93; Howard and, xxii; Poker
    Joe and, 59–60, 134n15; surrender
    of, xviii–xix

Kenck, Charles, x, 70, *73*, 74, 75, 77;
    burial of, 85, 89–91, 115; shooting
    and death of, 76, 110; Stewart and,
    108; Stone and, 108

Lake Yellowstone, 37–38; Helena
    Party at, 80; Radersburg Party at,
    41–42, 52–53
Lakota, xviii
Lamar River, 42; Soda Butte and, 43
laundry, in geysers, 49–50
Lava Creek, 84
Lawyer, xix
Lean Elk. *See* Poker Joe
Lewis and Clark Expedition, xix
Liberty Cap, 89
Little Bighorn. *See* Battle of the Little
    Bighorn
locusts, 14, 131n1
Lolo Canyon, 7, 20
Lolo Pass, 68
Lolo Trail, xxi
Looking Glass, xii, 21, 29; death of,
    xviii; Poker Joe and, 134n15
Lower Falls, *100*; Cowan, G., at, 126;
    Helena Party at, 70; Radersburg

Party at, 53, 99; Sherman, W.,
    at, 10
Lower Geyser Basin, 40; Cowan, G.,
    at, 44–56, 119–20, 122; Nez Perce
    at, 3, 9, 58–67; Radersburg Party
    at, 44–56, 58–67; Sawtell's road
    to, 46

Madison Canyon, 22
Madison Mountain Range, 21
Madison River, 19, 21; Gibbon on,
    27–28; Helena Party on, 77; Nez
    Perce on, 30, 35; Oldham on, 121
Madison Valley, 33
Mammoth Hot Springs: Cowan, E.,
    at, 16–17; Dietrich to, 76; Helena
    Party at, 4, 42, 70, 76–77, 82, 87,
    111; Huston to, 53; Kenck to,
    75; Radersburg Party at, 99, 104;
    Sherman, W., at, 10, 11; Shively
    at, 43; Stone at, 114; Yellow Wolf
    at, 89
Mammoth Terraces, 70
Mann, Charles, ix, 17, 23; Cowan, G.,
    and, 119
March to the Sea, of Sherman, W., 5
Mary Mountain, 40, 49, 62
Mary Mountain Pass: Helena Party
    in, 80; Radersburg Party in, 62,
    64, 92
McCartney, James, xiii; cabin of, 1–4,
    11, 42, 43, 83, *88*, 97, 104, 111–12;
    Weikert and, 3, 84, 85–87, 89
Meyers, Henry, ix, 17, 19, 23; injury
    from geyser of, 46–47

Midway Geyser Basin, 38

Miles, Nelson A., xi, xviii, xxiii; at Battle of Bear Paws, xxi; at Fort Buford, 6

Missouri River, 19

Montana: buffalo in, 7, 68; Cowan, E., in, 14; forts in, 6; Nez Perce to, xxi, 1, 30. *See also specific locations*

Montana Column, 31

Mount Washburn: Helena Party at, 70, 83, 84; Radersburg Party at, 99; Schofield and, 103; Sherman, W., at, 10

Mud Geyser, 41; Radersburg Party at, 51

Mud Springs, 126

Mud Volcano, xxiii

Nez Perce: alliances of, 68; at Battle of Bear Paws, xxi; at Big Hole River, xviii, xxi, 8, 11–13, 21, 29, 30, 47, 69; to Bitterroot Valley, 7–8, 12, 21; to Canada, xviii; Christianity of, xix; Cowan, E., and, 55; on Firehole River, 58; Fort Missoula and, 29; in Gallatin Valley, 13; Helena Party and, 4, 74–78; at Henderson's Ranch, 88; at Henrys Lake, 30, 33–35, 58; horses and, 29–30, 35, 42, 58, 92, 118–19; Howard and, 69; Lewis and Clark Expedition and, xix; at Lolo Canyon, 7, 20; at Lower Geyser Basin, 3, 9, 58–67; on Madison River, 35; McCartney's cabin and, 1–4; to

Montana, xxi, 1, 30; Radersburg Party and, 40–41, 55–67, 92–107, 134n8; on reservation, xix; scouts' search for, 29–36; Sherman, W., and, 1–2; Shively and, 39–42, 64; in Targhee Pass, 35; at Tolo Lake, xxi; in Yellowstone Park, xxi–xxii, 5, 40, 69; at Yellowstone River, *34*, 79–80, 96

Nez Perce Creek, 50, 133n2; into Firehole River, 62

Nez Perce Joseph (Howard), xxii

Norris, Philetus W., 46

Old Faithful: Radersburg Party at, 47–49; Sherman, W., at, 10–11

Oldham, Albert, ix, 17, 22; capture of, 64; injury of, 26; at Lower Geyser Basin, 55; shooting of, 65, 104, 121–22

Omohundro, John Baker "Texas Jack," xiii, 54; at Bottlers Ranch, *127*; Cody and, 51; at McCartney's cabin, 2, 111; Radersburg Party and, 99, 104, 105–6

"The only good Indian is a dead Indian.," 86

Otter Creek: Helena Party at, 80, 85; into Yellowstone River, 74

Owl Creek Range, 37

Paradise Valley, Bottlers Ranch in, *9*; Cowan, G., at, 126, 129; Radersburg Party at, 106, *127*; Sherman, W., to, 9–10

Parker, Frank J., 123

peace council, xxi

Pfister, Frederic, x, 69, *72*, 76, *80*; to
Fort Ellis, 105; to McCartney's
cabin, 83; Radersburg Party and,
103–4

pidgin English, xxii, 98, 133n5

Poe, O. M., xii, 11, 134n2

Poker Joe, xii, xxiii; Arnold and,
63–64; at Battle of Bear Paws, 98;
Big Hole River and, 57; Carpenter,
F., and, 64, 97–98, 99, 134n15;
Carpenter, I., and, 94; Cowan, E.,
and, 96, 97; death of, 98; Dingee
and, 63–64; Joseph and, 59–60;
Radersburg Party and, 57–67;
Shively and, 40–42, 63

Potts, Benjamin F., 5, 7–8

Radersburg Party, ix, *18*; at Bottlers
Ranch, 106, *127*; capture of, 40–41,
57–67, 92–107; on Firehole River,
50, 62; Helena Party and, 104–5;
at Henrys Lake, 22–26, 62; horses
of, 53, 55, 63; at Lake Yellowstone,
41–42, 52–53; at Lower Falls, 99;
at Lower Geyser Basin, 44–56,
58–67; at Mammoth Hot Springs,
99, 104; in Mary Mountain Pass,
92; at McCartney's cabin, 83, 104;
Nez Perce and, 40–41, 55–67,
92–107, 134n8; at Old Faithful,
47–49; Omohundro and, 99, 104,
105–6; Poker Joe and, 57–67;
Sherman, W., and, 26–27; Shively

and, 37–43, 50; at Upper Geyser
Basin, 38, 47–48; at Yellowstone
Falls, 53, 98; to Yellowstone Park,
14–28; Yellow Wolf and, 55–56,
58–60. *See also specific members*

Rawn, Charles, 7–8

Raynolds Pass, 22

Reddington, J. W., 120

Reno, Marcus, 30

reservations: Cheyenne on, 31; Crow
Indians on, 106; Nez Perce on, xix;
Sioux on, 31

Roberts, Joe, 68–78, *72*, *80*; Dietrich
and, 84; Foller and, 77–78, 115; to
Virginia City, 89, 114

Rocky Canyon, 129

Rosebud (steamboat), 5–6

Sawtell, Gilman, 16, 21; road of, 22,
26, 47; stories of, 44; village of,
23–26

Schofield, Robert, 101–4; Fort Ellis
and, 103, 104, 105

Scott, Hugh Lenox, xii, 88, 89, 126

Sheridan, Philip, 86

Sherman, Tom, 9, 11

Sherman, William Tecumseh, xii,
5–13; Arnold and, 123; Cowan, E.,
and, 54; at Fort Ellis, 7, 11–12, 70;
Herendeen and, 30; at Mammoth
Hot Springs, 10, 11; March to the
Sea by, 5; at McCartney's cabin, 1,
11; Nez Perce and, 1–2; to Paradise
Valley, 9–10; Radersburg Party and,
26–27; on *Rosebud*, 5–6; Sioux and,

6; at Tower Fall, 10; Upper Geyser Basin and, 5, 11; to Yellowstone Park, 8

Shively, John, xiii, 2–3; Cowan, E., and, 97; gold and, 37–38; at Mammoth Hot Springs, 43; to McCartney's cabin, 4; Nez Perce and, 39–42, 64; Poker Joe and, 40–42, 63; Radersburg Party and, 37–43, 50; Yellow Wolf and, 58

Shoshone Indians, 37

Sioux, 68; at Battle of the Little Bighorn, 101; Montana Column and, 31; to reservations, 31; Sherman, W., and, 6

Sitting Bull, xviii, 5

Snake Indians, 42

Snake River, 23; Henrys Fork of, 30; Shively at, 37

Soda Butte, 43

Spanish Peaks, 21

Spurgeon (Captain), 126

Sterling, 20, 21

Stewart, John, x, 70, 76, 82–83; horse of, 110–11; Kenck and, 108; Radersburg Party and, 104–5; shooting of, 82, 110; Stone and, 108–9, 111; Weikert and, 82–83, 111; Wilkie and, 111–12

Stone, Ben, x, 70, 73, 79, 82, 83; Duncan and, 75–76; escape of, 108–15; to Henderson's Ranch, 113, 114; Kenck and, 108; at Mammoth Hot Springs, 114; at McCartney's cabin, 112;

Radersburg Party and, 104; Stewart and, 108–9, 111; Weikert and, 89

Stoner, Jake, 112, 114, 115

Story, Nelson, xiv, 50–51; at Lower Geyser Basin, 54

Sulphur Mountain: Helena Party at, 71; Radersburg Party at, 53

Targhee Pass, 26, 30; Nez Perce in, 35

Texas Jack. See Omohundro, John Baker

Tobacco Root Mountains, 20

Tolo Lake, xxi

Toohoolhoolzote, xviii, xxi

Tower Creek, 99

Tower Fall, 3; Cowan, E., at, 102; Helena Party at, 70; Radersburg Party at, 99; Sherman, W., at, 10

Trail Creek Pass, 9, 129; Helena Party at, 11–12

Undine Falls, 84

Upper Falls: Helena Party at, 70; Sherman, T., at, 11

Upper Geyser Basin: Radersburg Party at, 38, 47–48; Sherman, W., and, 5, 11

Virginia City, 57; Bean and Herendeen in, 35–36; Cowan, E., in, 14–16; Foller, August to, 89, 115; Helena Party in, 78; Henrys Lake to, 22; Roberts to, 89, 114

Weikert, Andrew, x, 70–71, *72*, 75, 76, 79–82, *80*, 88; Dietrich and, 83, 84, 89–90; McCartney and, 3, 84, 85–87, 89; at McCartney's cabin, 3–4, 83; Radersburg Party and, 104–5; shooting of, 81; Stewart and, 82–83, 111; Stone and, 89

White Bird, xxi, 134n15

Wilkie, Leslie, xi, 70, 74, 75, 76, 80–82, 88; Radersburg Party and, 104; Stewart and, 111–12

The Wonders of Geyser Land (Carpenter, F.), xxii

Wood (prospector), 27

Yellowstone Falls: Helena Party at, 70–71, 74, 75, 84; Radersburg Party at, 53, 98

Yellowstone Park: Bottler in, 9–10; Cowan, E., in, 16–17, *66*; Cowan, G., in, *66*; Nez Perce in, xxi–xxii, 5, 40, 69; Radersburg Party to, 14–28; Sherman, W., to, 8; specimen collecting ban in, 46. *See also specific locations*

Yellowstone River: Helena Party on, 74; Nez Perce at, *34*, 79–80, 96; Otter Creek into, 74; Radersburg Party at, 99; Sherman, W., at, 7; Shively on, 38

Yellow Wolf, xii, 2–3; Dietrich and, 88–89; at Mammoth Hot Springs, 89; Radersburg Party and, 55–56, 58–60; Shively and, 39

About the Author

M. Mark Miller is a fifth-generation Montanan who grew up on a cattle ranch in southwest Montana about ninety miles from Yellowstone Park. His interest in early park travel began when he was a little boy listening to his grandmother's tales of cooking bread in hot springs and throwing red flannel underwear into geysers to tint the next eruption pink.

He worked for Montana newspapers while in college at the University of Montana. After graduating, he was a reporter and editor for newspapers in Utah and Kentucky. He earned a doctorate and became a journalism professor at the universities of Wisconsin and Tennessee.

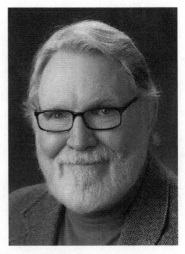

WINSLOW STUDIO

Miller returned home to Montana in 2003. He has been researching Yellowstone Park history since then and has a collection of more than four hundred first-person accounts of early travel to Yellowstone Park. TwoDot has published two of his anthologies of such accounts: *Adventures in Yellowstone: Early Travelers Tell the Tales*, and *The Stories of Yellowstone: Adventure Tales from the World's First National Park*. In addition, he has published *Macon's Perfect Shot*, a mid-grades novel about a fourteen-year-old boy's adventures in Yellowstone Park in 1871.

Miller's articles on Yellowstone Park and Montana history have appeared in *Montana Quarterly*, *Big Sky Journal*, and the *Gallatin History Quarterly* (formerly the *Pioneer Museum Quarterly*). He also lectures on park history to various civic groups.

He lives in Bozeman where he has been a volunteer at the Gallatin History Museum since 2004.